Sunset

BASIC GARDENING
ILLUSTRATED

By the Editors of Sunset Books and Sunset Magazine

LANE BOOKS • MENLO PARK, CALIF.

Foreword

Gardening is essentially an uncomplicated and relaxing activity. Nevertheless there are certain basic rules which, if not followed, can result in many avoidable mistakes. The home gardener who understands and uses the relatively few but all-important fundamentals will be rewarded by the kind of success that has caused gardening to become one of the most popular of all activities. When the correct steps are followed, gardening is really simple—and sure-fire.

With this in mind, we have edited this book with heavy emphasis on the easy, visual, how-to-do-it approach to everyday gardening. Drawings and photographs play the main role wherever possible. Text has been held to a minimum, although a few sections (such as fertilizers) contain detailed discussions of vital gardening subjects that do not readily lend themselves to illustration.

Here, then, is a book which will serve not only as a primer for the beginner, but as a valuable reference for home gardeners everywhere. As a "no-nonsense" hand-book for people who have neither the time nor the inclination to garden any more than they have to, this volume fills a long-felt need. Additionally, much of the subject matter will appeal to those more experienced green-thumbers who wish to improve on their techniques or to try their hand at grafting, budding, or some other procedure which may have mystified them in the past.

The first ten chapters are concerned entirely with general gardening techniques. The final three, beginning on page 95, picture and describe the basic garden plants, including certain specific cultural needs. We have organized the book in this fashion so as to avoid needless repetition of techniques that pertain not just to one but to several kinds of plants. At the start of each chapter we have listed, for your convenience, the subjects covered therein, along with their page numbers. However, in order that you may get the most from this book, we urge you to make a habit of referring to the index (pages 126 through 128). The thorough cross-indexing will help you to find quickly and easily the information you need.

ACKNOWLEDGMENTS

Much of the material in this book has appeared in the gardening pages of *Sunset,* the Magazine of Western Living. Additionally, considerable information was compiled especially for the book. We wish to thank the dozens of consultants— nurserymen, growers, scientists, and garden specialists—for their advice and co-operation. Also, we extend a special thanks to commercial artist E. D. Bills for the hundreds of clear and accurate sketches which appear throughout these pages.

Executive Editor, Sunset Books: David E. Clark

Eighteenth Printing April 1973

CHAPTER 1

Understanding Your Soil

DARROW M. WATT

HEAVY VERSUS LIGHT SOILS

It's a rare gardener that is completely satisfied with the physical nature of his soil. Typically, the soil is either too sticky when wet and too hard when dry, or is too sandy and must be watered too often. Strangely enough, in many cases the same prescription cures both of these opposite ills.

TOO CLAYEY

The flat, plate-like particles that make up a clay soil are so minute that the largest is only about 1/25 as large as the smallest particle of sand. When there is little organic matter in a clay soil, these particles fit together very closely, with little air space between them.

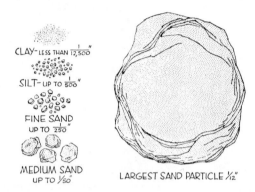

When such a soil gets wet, it dries slowly because movement of water down through the soil is obstructed (poor drainage), and circulation of air within the soil is seriously hampered (poor aeration). As a result root growth is severely inhibited.

In the worst clay soils, plants that manage to struggle along are stunted and the root systems are shallow (because the roots will grow only where there is an adequate supply of oxygen)—despite the fact that the individual clay particles are well supplied with the nutrients essential for plant growth.

TOO SANDY

Conditions in a sandy soil are quite different. The rounded but irregular sand particles resemble tiny boulders: Although one particle rests against another, large air spaces remain. Aeration is excellent—usually too good.

As a result of this aeration, plus very free drainage, the soil dries rapidly. Nutrients, mostly in solution, leach away quickly because of the frequent watering required and the

sand's lack of nutrient-retentive properties. A sandy soil, therefore, needs feeding at frequent intervals.

CULTIVATING

Although cultivating has very little effect on sandy soils, cultivating heavy clay soil with either a rotary tiller or a spade temporarily improves its structure by improving aeration. But if it is wet, a heavy clay soil can be harmed more than helped by cultivation, because soil particles are simply packed closer together, driving out the air.

Improved aeration of heavy clay soils creates a climate suitable for plant root growth because air (or oxygen) is essential to growth. Temporarily, roots can live in the soil and freely absorb the clay's abundance of nutrients. But the benefits of cultivation are rapidly lost as the soil gradually compacts again upon exposure to weathering, continued watering, and foot traffic.

SOIL AMENDMENTS

However, if you add a soil amendment at the time you cultivate a clay soil, you supply it with long-lasting air spaces. The same treatment helps sandy soil in a different way. For such amendments contain plenty of air and a great capacity for holding it (porosity), plus the ability to hold moisture. The air holding capacity of a soil amendment is significant in heavy clays; the moisture holding capacity is significant in very sandy soils.

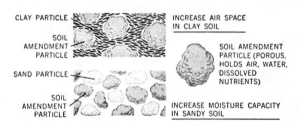

Any material that in itself is a good plant growing medium, when water and plant food are added, can be considered a good soil amendment. Several of these are being offered to the home gardener now. These can be classed as mineral and organic. Mineral amendments include perlite, pumice, and vermiculite. Some of the most popular organic amendments are ground bark, sawdust, leaf mold, manure, and peat moss.

The greater quantity of soil amendment you mix into the soil, the more you increase its air and moisture holding capacity. Mixing must be uniform and the resulting medium homogeneous. The initial effect is purely physical (dilution of the clay or sand particles with the soil amendment). You're actually mixing a good growing medium with one that is only fair or poor. When decomposable organic amendments are added to clay soils, something else also happens—a breakdown causes aggregation of particles (more about that below).

If you want to make a marked improvement in a problem soil, you must add a volume of soil amendment equal to 25 to 50 per cent of the total soil volume in the cultivated area. This means that in a 100-cubic-foot area, you'll need from 50 to 100 cubic feet of soil amendment (loosened, not compacted volume as with tightly baled peat moss). After you mix it in, your soil level will naturally be higher; remember, however, that it will eventually pack down considerably.

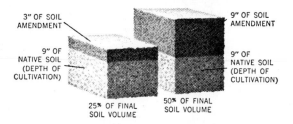

Manure often has a high salt content which would damage the roots if added in these large quantities. So you should limit the quantities of manure to about 5 or 6 (no more than 8) cubic feet per 100 cubic feet of soil.

Perlite, pumice, and vermiculite remain virtually unaltered in the soil except for gradual decomposition caused by weathering. On the other hand, organic soil amendments are gradually broken down by the action of soil micro-organisms, to form humus. Humus, a gelatinous material, surrounds clay particles and acts as a glue binding large groups of soil particles together into aggregates. In clay soils, aggregation improves aeration and drainage, and plant roots can grow through the soil with easy access to the nutrient elements—held by soil particles and organic matter.

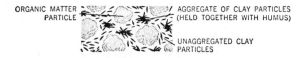

In sandy soils, good aeration speeds up the decomposition of organic soil amendments. It's preferable, therefore, to use a mineral amendment or one of the slower decomposing materials such as peat moss, ground bark, sawdust, spent hops or some other locally available waste product, for a more lasting moisture and nutrient-holding capacity.

The soil micro-organisms require a constant supply of nitrogen to break down the organic matter. They get this nitrogen from the soil, or from nitrogen fertilizers, and from organic matter that we add to the soil. It's best not to depend upon the nitrogen already present in the soil (an unknown quantity unless you've had specific tests made).

Any organic material that contains at least 1.5 per cent nitrogen has enough to take care of its own decomposition without reducing the total nitrogen supply in the soil. A reduction in this supply could bring plant growth to a standstill.

Leaves and leaf mold, peat moss, and garden compost almost always contain sufficient quantities of nitrogen to provide for their own decomposition. With the addition of fir, pine, and redwood sawdust or bark (composted or with nitrogen added), it's usually not necessary to add more nitrogen to the soil. Some of these materials, however, either haven't been composted long enough or haven't had sufficient nitrogen added, and so draw upon and temporarily deplete the soil's nitrogen while undergoing decomposition. Addition of 25 to 50 per cent of dried leaves or leaf mold could temporarily deplete the soil's nitrogen but doesn't necessitate addition of more nitrogen to the soil, because this temporary depletion lasts for a very short time and the nitrogen is soon released again. Addition of nitrogenous fertilizer could result in damage from too much nitrogen.

When you add fresh fir, pine, or redwood sawdust or bark to the soil (not composted or fortified with nitrogen), soil nitrogen is temporarily depleted. Raw redwood sawdust and bark, and fir and pine bark, impose the least problem with soil fertility because they only partially decompose. For every cubic foot of these materials that you add to the soil, also include about 3 ounces of blood meal or hoof and horn meal, or 1 ounce of ammonium sulfate.

Raw pine and fir sawdust decompose almost completely, markedly decreasing the soil nitrogen supply in the process. Make the same fertilizer application as suggested above, and then watch plant growth for danger signs from nitrogen depletion (leaves will turn yellow). If these signs develop, make a second application. These nitrogen applications supplement the regular feedings made to nourish the plants growing in this soil.

Keep in mind that humus itself breaks down and is lost to the soil, especially in well aerated, well drained soil (two favorable conditions that the addition of organic matter helps to create).

Therefore organic matter must be added, in smaller quantities, at regular intervals. Turning in a 1 to 2-inch organic mulch at the end of each growing season satisfies this demand.

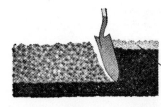

1" TO 2" ORGANIC MULCH TURNED UNDER EACH YEAR (MAINTAINS ORGANIC MATTER LEVEL AND TILTH)

WORKING THE SOIL TAKES KNOW-HOW

There's a special language, spoken by gardeners, nurserymen, and garden writers, that's a sort of jargon of the trade. It's full of words and expressions that are puzzling to beginners and, quite frequently, not fully understood by more experienced gardeners.

For example, during the spring planting months you find this kind of advice in print almost everywhere: "A week before you plan to plant, cultivate the planting bed deeply, and add generous amounts of humus, mixing it thoroughly with the soil. Your purpose is to get a soil that is friable, crumbly, well drained, and well aerated."

This is perfectly good garden language, but it's written in shorthand. It attempts to describe the total process of preparing the soil for planting. Analyze that paragraph and you can see that there could be almost as many meanings as there are gardeners. Look at these words and terms: *cultivate, generous, friable, well drained*. What do they mean?

A study of the illustrations below, plus the information on the preceding 2 pages, will do more than merely clarify these terms; it will give you some basic know-how that can help you in nearly all of your gardening endeavors.

Cultivation is more than just "digging" . . .

Plant roots *cultivate soil naturally—better than any tools. They create passageways, add humus to soil when they die.*

This is the wrong way *to cultivate around a plant. Cultivate shallowly where there is danger of cutting or exposing roots.*

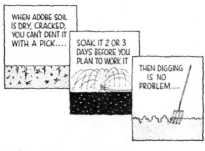

Adobe soil, *prevalent in many areas, is hard to work with when too dry or wet. Friable stage (above) is best time to dig.*

When spading in manure *or other soil amendments, turn each spadeful on its side rather than upside-down.*

Cultivate *crusted soil in fall to reduce surface run-off in winter. Add soil amendments to condition beds for spring.*

Power cultivator *does thorough job of mixing in soil amendments. Fertilizer can also be mixed in at this time.*

Friable *is described by dictionary as "easily crumbled." To test for friability, ball up a fistful of soil. If compressed soil stays balled, it is too wet to dig and probably too heavy. If it is just dry enough to crumble, it is friable.*

For thorough blending *of large amounts of mix spread organic material over soil, and throw spadefuls of it and soil into a pile. Move pile a spadeful at a time to second pile, throwing the mix so it runs down the pile, blending as it goes.*

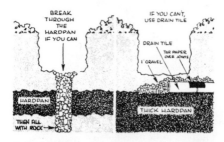

Soil drainage *may be poor even though surface drainage (movement of excess water over soil surface) is excellent. A rock-filled drain hole cannot do an effective job unless it goes through to a layer of soil that drains water fast.*

SOIL PROBLEMS

Almost every gardener has a soil problem of one kind or another. Sometimes the problem is quite obvious; more likely than not, however, he is either unaware of the problem or does not fully understand it.

County agents, nurserymen, and experienced local gardeners can be helpful in testing or evaluating your soil. Do-it-yourself soil testing kits are widely available, and will give you a good idea—if not the total answer—of the status of your soil.

The six soil problems discussed below are by no means the only ailments to be found, but they are ones which home gardeners should be aware of. Complete books have been written about most of them; here, we can list only fundamental information to acquaint the reader with their basic symptoms and cures.

Alkalinity

Alkaline soil, common in light-rainfall areas of California and some other parts of the West, is soil that is high in calcium carbonate (lime) and certain other minerals. Many plants will grow well in a moderately alkaline soil, although camellias and other acid-loving plants will not thrive.

Areas with softened water are quite likely to have alkaline soil. The sodium in soft water is good for household use but poor for the garden. Hard water, on the other hand, is ideal for garden watering.

Large-scale chemical treatment of extremely alkaline soils is expensive and complex. A better bet is to plant in a good soil mix, in raised beds and containers.

Salinity

An excess of salt in the soil is a widespread problem in arid and semi-arid regions. It can prevent germination; or, if plants are already growing, it stunts them and in advanced cases burns the foliage and finally kills them. Its presence can usually be detected by a white deposit of salt on the surface of the soil. Frequent and shallow watering, as well as fertilizers, can cause salts to build up. Periodic and thorough leaching will help.

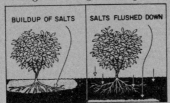

BUILDUP OF SALTS — SALTS FLUSHED DOWN

Chlorosis

Chlorosis is a plant ailment caused by inability of plants to take in iron from the soil through their root systems. If the deficiency is mild, areas of yellow show up between the veins of the leaf; if the deficiency is severe, the entire leaf except the veins turns yellow.

Iron deficiency in the plant is only occasionally the result of deficient amounts of iron in the soil; more frequently it is the result of some other substance (principally lime) that renders the iron unavailable.

Chemical treatment of the soil with chelating agents (pronounced kee-lating) or with iron sulfate can correct a chlorosis condition. They are available at many nurseries and garden stores.

Acidity

Acid soil is at the other end of the scale from alkaline soil. It is most common in areas of heavy rainfall, and is often associated with sandy soil (in the latter case, ocean beach areas are an exception).

Mildly acid soils cause little trouble, but an intense acid condition is highly undesirable for most plants.

Liming materials will help to neutralize an acid-reacting soil, since all acid soils are low in calcium (lime). Your choice of fertilizers can be another very important factor in controlling acidity; some fertilizers can actually increase soil acidity.

Some plants—azaleas, rhododendrons, and camellias to name a few —actually prefer soil that is moderately acid in reaction.

Nutrient deficiency

Most soils, left to themselves, yield the three major plant nutrients—nitrogen, phosphorus, and potassium—very slowly. Even the richest soil cannot continue to provide an ample amount of these vital elements year after year.

Fertilizers—either chemical or organic—are the quickest and easiest answer to a nutrient deficiency. Many balanced fertilizers, containing all three major elements, are available (see the chapter beginning on page 51). There are also formulations of nitrogen, phosphorus, or potassium compounds that provide these single nutrients.

Manure and finely ground compost are also beneficial in varying degrees to nutrient-shy soils, but are more effective in their ability to build up the soil's humus supply.

Shallow soil (hardpan)

If your soil changes to a layer of hardpan or more impervious material within the top 18 inches, you are in for some trouble. Roots won't go down as deeply as they should; the main problem, however, is soil drainage. Every time you set out a plant that roots deeply, drill through the tough layer with an auger. Refill the excavated portion with gravel.

CLAY
HARDPAN
GRAVEL

If the hardpan layer is too thick, a landscape engineer can help you install a special drain system. Switching to raised bed and container gardening is another possibility.

MIXING A BATCH OF POTTING SOIL

Mixing potting soil is not always the large-scale operation shown below. Many gardeners, when they decide to pot up a plant or two, simply pick up a trowel and mix a small quantity of whatever they need at the moment. Or, they buy a sack of ready-to-use mix at the nursery.

However, if you do a large amount of container gardening or if you are putting in some raised beds, a little shovel-and-wheelbarrow work is called for.

Good potting soil should contain sufficient nutrients for plant growth and development; it should be easy to work, and easy for roots to penetrate; and it should be sufficiently porous for water to penetrate it thoroughly, yet not so open that water runs through it too rapidly.

A popular basic mixture consists of 2 parts good garden loam, 1 part sand, and 1 part peat moss or the equivalent. (You may also wish to add bonemeal or other fertilizer.) This formula is subject to endless variations, depending mainly on two things: 1) The character of the loam; and, 2) the kinds of plants you intend to grow.

If you have a sandy loam, omit the 1 part sand and use 3 parts sandy loam. Whatever you do, never use clayey soil in a container mix.

Certain plants—azaleas, camellias, and rhododendrons for example—will not do their best unless the mix consists of at least 50% organic matter such as finely ground bark, peat moss, or leaf mold.

At potting time, the mix should be damp but not wet. A good test for dampness is the same as the standard one for soil texture: squeeze a handful hard. If it falls apart quickly when the hand is opened, it is too dry; if any water comes out, it is too wet; if it retains its shape as squeezed and merely cracks slightly, it is damp enough.

The photographs below show one of the many variations of the U.C. Mix, an artificial soil that is popular with many growers and home gardeners in the West. It consists of sand and peat moss or ground bark, plus nutrients. Although the ingredients may be different, you follow the same procedure to make any soil mix.

1. *If you use peat moss in mix, first water it with a hose, then thoroughly knead in moisture with your hands.*

2. *First blending: Throw alternate shovelfuls of organic material, soil and/or sand into mixing pile (left foreground).*

3. *Second blending: Retoss layered pile from first blending into new pile (rear). Flat shovel works well on patio surface.*

4. *If you wish to add bonemeal or other nutrients (U.C. Mix uses several), spread them evenly over flattened pile.*

5. *Blend nutrients with mix by tossing over a shovelful at a time into new pile; for best results, repeat process.*

DARROW M. WATT

6. *Mixture is now ready to use. U.C. Mix, pictured here, is described in Sunset book, Gardening in Containers.*

RAISED BEDS

Raised beds can be the salvation of the gardener who has perplexing soil problems—particularly if he is haunted by the bugaboo of poor drainage.

Even if your native soil is excellent, you may want some raised beds to highlight a spectacular planting, change levels, bring plants up close, supply built-in seating, interrupt the monotony of paving, or grow plants neatly against a building wall.

The soil mix you use depends on what you are planting (see the facing page for some examples). Be sure to check your raised bed's drainage features before you add soil. If the structure is open to the ground at the bottom, most excess water will drain out. If it's closed, make weep holes on the sides about 2 or 3 inches up from the base. Space them about 2 or 3 feet apart. It is also a good idea to place an 8 to 10-inch layer of crushed rock in the bottom before you fill in with a loose soil mixture.

Soak soil so it settles to a natural level. If you wait until after plants are in, many will sink and you'll have to lift and replant them. To keep water from spilling out, keep soil level 3 or 4 inches below top of the planter.

ROBERT COX

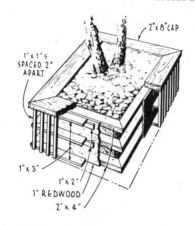

JOHN ROBINSON

Small tree *is showcased by raised bed measuring 4 feet by 6 feet. Landscape Architects: Eckbo, Royston & Williams.*

Raised bed *made from low redwood wall, 2 by 6-inch cap. Landscape Architects: Thomas Church and Associates.*

Construction materials and methods . . .

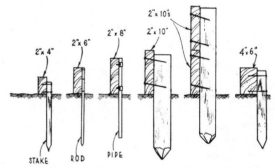

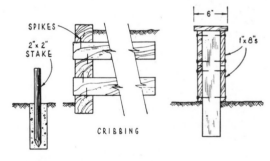

Rough-finish *redwood or cedar makes good looking low wall. It is easy to install, inexpensive, and weathers well. For best alignment, have one edge and one end of each board surfaced.*

A row of 2 by 2-inch stakes can be driven into ground, or embedded in a narrow trench filled with concrete, as shown above. Where wall is under heavy strain, cribbing adds strength.

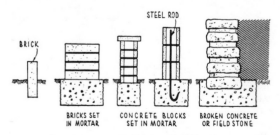

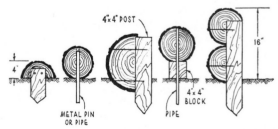

Masonry *makes strong, enduring wall if footings go down far enough and are heavy enough. To relieve water pressure, provide small holes for drainage through the wall.*

To get logs, you may have to go directly to woods with a truck or trailer and negotiate with loggers. Logs look especially good in an informal, shady setting with azaleas, fuchsias, begonias.

COMPOSTING . . . IS IT FOR YOU?

SIFT OUT FINISHED COMPOST BEFORE
YOU ADD RAW MATERIALS—

Compost can be a tremendous asset to any garden, if—and we repeat, if—it is developed carefully and diligently. A poorly maintained compost pile breeds enormous quantities of flies and other pests, and has an odor that can be obnoxious to both you and your neighbors.

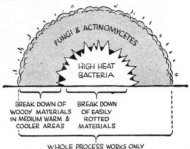

Turn compost pile *often to keep moisture, air, and microbe action in balance.*

Before you build a compost bin, ask yourself these questions:

1. Do I have a good, out-of-the-way location for a bin on my property?
2. Is the time and effort involved in proper upkeep really worth it to me, when it would cost only a few dollars a year for manure or other humus-building material?

If you can honestly answer "yes" on both questions, read on. If your answer is "no" to either of them, you are better off to forget the whole idea.

Composting in its simplest form consists of piling up grass clippings, leaves, and other garden refuse, plus certain kitchen material such as coffee grounds—then allowing it to decompose. Later (usually 3 to 6 months) you spade it back into the garden, thus adding nutrients and humus to the soil.

There are innumerable improvements on this procedure, of course. The first improvement is putting the debris in an enclosed bin where you can work with it easier. All a bin amounts to is a way of enclosing raw material while microbes work on it.

The compost heap should be turned every week (or oftener) with a spading fork or pitchfork, to put air into the center and to relocate material in the various phases of decomposition. The whole compost-making process can be carried out successfully only if there is a balance of moisture, air, and microbe action. At the bottom of the pile, near the center, high heat bacteria go to work on soft, easily rotted material. Fungi and actinomycetes bacteria are at work in the rest of the pile.

To sift and load *compost in one operation, lean the screen against a wheelbarrow.*

When compost becomes crumbly and ready to use, sift it through a 1-inch wire screen or sieve for general garden use. A ½-inch screen is preferable if you want finer textured compost for potting or as a lawn dressing.

IF YOUR COMPOST BIN IS SO FULL IT'S ABOUT TO SPLIT IT'S SIDES....SPREAD SOME OF THE SURPLUS (OR NEW MATTER FROM FALL CLEANUP) OVER THE GROUND IN 2" TO 3" LAYERS—SPADE IT IN NEXT SPRING (DON'T USE WOODY MATERIAL THAT WON'T DECAY)

Sheet composting *is popular with some gardeners as a means of putting surplus undecayed matter to good use.*

SIMPLE COMPOST BIN

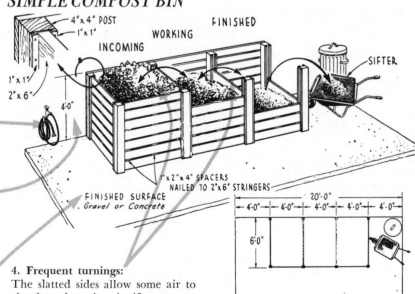

This compost receptacle illustrates physical features that help make fast compost without aid of soil or manure. Many bins and boxes now in existence can be worked by this method.

1. Water always handy:
Hose and sprinkler supply water that keeps fast-working compost damp as a squeezed sponge.

2. Optimum height 4 to 6 feet:
If a pile is too low, heat is lost rapidly and composting action slows. If too high, the weight will compress the material, cut off vital air and make too much heat.

3. Place to handle raw material:
Material should be walnut-size chunks or smaller. Space allows for temporary stacking to await any necessary grinding, chopping.

4. Frequent turnings:
The slatted sides allow some air to circulate, but the significant aeration comes with frequent turnings (every 2 or 3 days for best results). This set of bins is designed for easy access with spading fork.

Outer surface is 4 feet wide to give gardener plenty of working room.

CHAPTER 2

Propagating Techniques

CLYDE CHILDRESS

STARTING SEEDS IN GROUND

Many annuals, and some biennials and perennials, can be grown very successfully from seed sown directly in the open ground. Generally speaking, you'll have healthier plants and an earlier and longer bloom period if you plant in this fashion—especially with the faster kinds of summer annuals. The shock of transplanting is entirely eliminated.

There is one minor disadvantage in that your seeded garden bed will display no flower color during the 6 weeks or more that it takes the seeds to germinate and reach maturity. Against this, many gardens are bursting with color from bulbs and other spring-blooming plants at the time most annuals should be seeded, and a bed or two of seedlings will constitute no great deficit.

Be sure to follow seed packet directions as to planting time for your region.

Spring is the best time to plant, but wait until frost danger is past and soil has begun to warm up; soil should be just at the crumbly stage and not too wet.

Some of the many annuals that like to be planted in open ground are: sweet alyssum, aster, coreopsis, gaillardia, marigold, nasturtium, phlox, portulaca, and zinnia.

The method below is one good way to sow seed, but many gardeners prefer to sow in rows. The same principles of culture should be followed with either method.

1. *Spread 3 inches of peat moss or other conditioner over seed bed, plus fertilizer. If soil is heavy, include 10 pounds gypsum per 100 square feet.*

2. *Spade these materials in well, to depth of 6 or 8 inches. Break clods with back of shovel. Rake level. (Optional: Apply a fungicide at this time.)*

3. *Work out a planting plan for the various annuals, arranging according to height. Outline areas with white powdered material such as gypsum or flour.*

4. *Place seed in a 1-pound coffee can. Add dry sand or peat moss until 2/3 full. Replace top; shake can to mix seed.*

5. *Broadcast seed, one kind at a time, within proper areas; firm with back of rake. Cover with 1/4-inch peat moss.*

6. *Water gently and evenly with a fine mist; avoid puddling. If slugs or snails are problem, apply bait.*

7. *After 2 pairs of true leaves develop, thin crowded areas by removing or transplanting. Leave plants minimum distance apart in hot areas (roots get more shade).*

8. *Feed every 2 weeks with high-nitrogen liquid fertilizer (sprinkle to wash off foliage afterward). Switch to complete fertilizer after flower buds form.*

9. *After plants are established, water by irrigating. Frequent overhead watering sometimes encourages disease; also, plants may sag under water's weight.*

STARTING SEEDS IN FLATS

Even if you like to sow some annuals directly where they are to grow (see facing page) you may wish to start some seeds indoors. There are certain advantages: It's the best method to use for expensive or very fine seed, for seed that takes a long time to germinate and grow (including most perennials), and for some annuals and vegetables that you want to start early when the ground outside is still too cold or wet. You can control the soil mix, you can move the flats or pots around so plants get the right amount of sun or shade, and pest damage is more quickly noticeable and easier to control.

New commercial refinements on the seed-starting process are being developed constantly, most of which are highly worthwhile and readily available to home gardeners. For example, seed starter kits are an ingenious shortcut: All you do is remove the lid of the container and add water. Seed, humus, and nutrients are all in the compact container. The seeding medium is sterile, so you don't have to worry about damping-off disease.

You can also buy tiny pots made of compressed peat moss, manure, or similar materials. Seedlings started in them can be planted pot and all at the proper planting time. Roots will grow right through the nutrient-filled walls of the pot, and will suffer no transplanting shock.

Here, we describe the long-popular method of starting and growing seeds in flats. Whether you use this procedure or one of the newer variations, the principles should help you to understand the basic fundamentals of starting seeds in containers.

WHEN TO SOW

You have to wait about 2½ to 4 months to get bloom from most annuals started from seed in April; this includes 8 to 10 weeks in the flat, from the time you sow seed until the plants are ready to set out in the garden. You have to plan

PLAN AHEAD—
IT TAKES FROM 2½ TO 4 MONTHS FOR MOST ANNUALS TO BLOOM FROM SEED

ahead. Get seed started as soon as possible; time your efforts so the plants are ready to set out at the right time. But it's not a good idea to hold them back by keeping them in too long in the flat.

SOIL PREPARATION

Most gardeners have their own pet mixes, but the important thing is to use a mix that is loose, drains well (won't cake like clay), yet holds moisture. Equal parts coarse river sand, peat moss or fine ground bark, and garden loam make a good basic mix. Screen it through a ¼-inch mesh.

To prevent damping-off (a soil disease that attacks seed and tiny seedlings), treat the seeding mixture (or the seed before it's sown) with a commercial fungicide. Some gardeners prefer to start seed in a sterile medium such as vermiculite.

HOW TO SOW

Fill the flat ½ to ¾ inch from the top with the seeding mix. Whether you use a flat or some other container such as a box or a pot, be sure there are holes or open spaces at the bottom for drainage.

Firm with a block of wood or the palm of your hand. Mark off rows (drills) with a piece of lath or a pencil, pressing ⅛ to

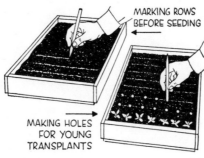

MARKING ROWS
BEFORE SEEDING

MAKING HOLES
FOR YOUNG
TRANSPLANTS

¼ inch deep into the mix. (If seed is fine, check the seed packet—most fine seeds should not be buried.) Space rows about 2 inches apart. Sow seeds in the little furrows and cover with sand, sifted peat moss, or sifted ground bark. Firm again so there's good contact between the seed and the mixture.

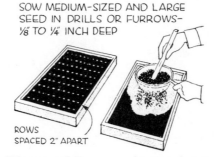

SOW MEDIUM-SIZED AND LARGE SEED IN DRILLS OR FURROWS— ⅛ TO ¼ INCH DEEP

ROWS
SPACED 2" APART

Water carefully so you don't wash out the seed. If you have a tub or sink, soak from below; otherwise, a small syringe comes in handy.

Label, then put a piece of wet burlap or wet newspaper over the surface. Cover the whole thing with a pane of glass if you have one handy; if not, just use the burlap or paper. Place the flat in a warm spot, but not in direct sun.

SEED GERMINATION

Keep the seeding mixture moist but not soaking wet. After 4 or 5 days, peek occasionally to see if seedlings have begun to appear. When the first ones show up, remove the newspaper or other cover; move flats into more light if they were in a fairly dark place. A lathhouse or a spot in the filtered sun under a tree is fine.

PRICKING OUT

This term simply means lifting the tiny seedlings when they have two sets of true leaves and moving them into another flat where they'll have room to develop. First fill flats with a slightly

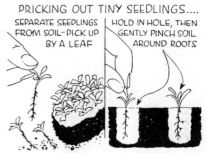

PRICKING OUT TINY SEEDLINGS....
SEPARATE SEEDLINGS FROM SOIL–PICK UP BY A LEAF | HOLD IN HOLE, THEN GENTLY PINCH SOIL AROUND ROOTS

richer mixture than the one in which you started the seed—a good one is 2 parts garden loam, one part river sand, and one part sifted peat moss or finely ground bark.

Lift and separate small clumps of seedlings with care. If roots are so lengthy that they would have to be doubled over in the planting hole, cut them back to a suitable length (but not too far).

Space seedlings about 1½ inches apart in the new flat. Water, and place the flat outdoors in the shade for 2 or 3 days to minimize possible shock before moving it into half sun.

Water plants occasionally—daily if weather is hot. A light weekly feeding with liquid fertilizer is a good extra step.

Several weeks later, when plants have put on enough growth so that their leaves touch those of the plant next to them, they are ready to be planted in their permanent location. (see page 28).

SEEDLINGS ARE READY TO SET OUT IN ABOUT 8 TO 10 WEEKS...

DIVIDING PERENNIALS

Each year the typical perennial gains in girth by growing new roots and stems, usually around the outer perimeter of the previous year's growth. Eventually (usually in 2 or 3 years) these clumps get too big for their space. Or perhaps growth has become weakened due to competition and crowding. It's time to divide the plant.

Each root segment or division is actually a plant in itself or is capable of becoming a new plant. Divide an overgrown clump into separate parts and you get that many new plants. It's a fast and inexpensive way of increasing your supply of favorite perennials.

Divide in autumn or early spring, when plants are dormant.

Fall is generally the best time to divide perennials that bloom in spring or early summer (in cold winter regions, this must be *early* fall). After dividing, keep roots moist and plant as soon as possible.

Deciduous and semi-deciduous perennials may be cut back to about 4 inches from the ground when you transplant. Young, healthy foliage of evergreens should not be cut back, but dead leaves should be removed. Woody plants such as marguerites can be pruned, but very lightly.

Here we show how to divide some of the various types of perennials. For information on how to grow and use perennials, see page 100.

Daylily. *To divide without cutting through many roots insert two forks in center of clump, spread handles. Use same method for acanthus, agapanthus, Siberian iris, poker plant.*

Divide *smaller daylily clumps with hand fork, knife, or hatchet. Unlike most evergreens, old leaves of daylilies may be cut back one-half. Don't cut the young center leaves.*

To prevent rot *later on—especially in heavy soil—dust roots of each daylily division with sulfur before replanting. Daylilies should be divided every 4 or 5 years.*

DARROW M. WATT

Columbine. *Divide every year or two by pulling apart carefully with hands, or by cutting through clump with sharp knife. Columbine also grows readily from seed.*

Coral bells. *Pull off separate divisions by hand. Discard old woody pieces; keep only the young vigorous sections. Divide clumps when they are about 3 to 5 years old.*

Make clean cut *across the bottom of each rooted division of coral bells. If mealybug is a problem in your region, dip the roots in a malathion solution before planting.*

Perennial candytuft. *Increase by dividing or by taking cuttings. Here you see a clump, a division, and several tip cuttings. Cuttings will root readily and grow quite rapidly.*

Perennial alyssum. *This one has tap roots, cannot be divided. Many gardeners grow perennial alyssum from seed; it germinates easily, gives blooming plants first year.*

Arabis. *Because of sparse roots and matted top growth, division is difficult. Instead, take 3-inch cuttings, insert in 4-inch pot of sand. Aubrieta is increased same way.*

Three months *after starting cuttings (see photo at left), you'll have a clump of arabis like this. Planted in fall, it will be a mass of snowy white bloom next spring.*

DIVIDING BULBOUS PLANTS

Bulbs have the same happy characteristic as perennials: Start with a few and in a few years you can have many—if you know how to go about it.

Two of the examples on this page are true bulbs; the rest are tubers, corms, or rhizomes—all of them generally considered members of the bulb family in a broad sense. Cultural characteristics of genera and species within each group are not identical, of course; but once you've divided iris, for example, you'll have little difficulty with óther rhizomes. The same is generally true of the other groups.

Daffodils

Daffodils and other members of the narcissus family can be left in the ground undisturbed for several years and still bloom freely each season. When flowers begin to get smaller and fewer in number, it's a sure sign that they are ready to be dug and divided.

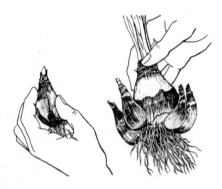

Don't dig until the bloom season is well past and foliage has dried and withered. You will find the mother bulb surrounded by several bulblets; remove only those which break away easily. Replant in fall.

Iris

Bearded iris and other types which grow from rhizomes begin to show signs of being crowded every 3 years or so. Divide them in late summer or early fall. Lift out root mass with a spading fork; then use a sharp knife to cut the new, growing rhizomes from the outer edge. Discard the rest.

DIVIDING

PLANTING DEPTH

GROWTH DIRECTION

DISCARD CENTER & UNDEVELOPED RHIZOMES

Dahlias

When early winter frosts turn dahlia foliage brown, it's time to dig and store the tubers. Whether you store the clumps for dividing next spring or divide them on the spot, be sure to let them dry out first. To divide, use a sharp knife and cut the new tubers so each has part of a crown attached to it and at least one dormant eye. Store them in dry sand or peat moss in a dry, cool place.

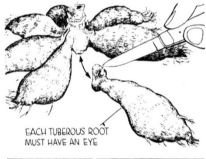

EACH TUBEROUS ROOT MUST HAVE AN EYE

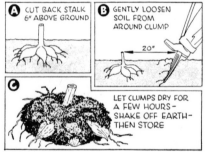

A. CUT BACK STALK 6" ABOVE GROUND

B. GENTLY LOOSEN SOIL FROM AROUND CLUMP — 20"

C. LET CLUMPS DRY FOR A FEW HOURS—SHAKE OFF EARTH—THEN STORE

Lilies

When lilies become crowded, lift in fall; cut away the old bulb at the bottom. If there are bulblets attached to the stem above it, replant—bulblets and all. Stem-rooting types have no bulblets.

Another way to increase lilies is to remove a few outer scales and plant them shallowly in a loose, well drained medium. In a year they'll be full sized.

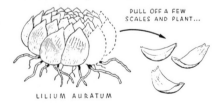

PULL OFF A FEW SCALES AND PLANT...

LILIUM AURATUM

Gladiolus

Gladiolus corms do best if they're lifted and stored each winter. Dig them well after bloom season, when leaves have turned a yellowish green.

Sometimes 2 large corms will have developed. Otherwise, you may wish to increase them by cutting them into halves or thirds. Also, cormels (see sketch immediately below) can be grown to full size in 2 or 3 years.

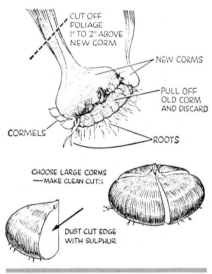

CUT OFF FOLIAGE 1" TO 2" ABOVE NEW CORM

NEW CORMS

PULL OFF OLD CORM AND DISCARD

CORMELS

ROOTS

CHOOSE LARGE CORMS —MAKE CLEAN CUTS

DUST CUT EDGE WITH SULPHUR

Tuberous begonias

Just before it's time to start tuberous begonias in spring (when shoots first appear), you can cut them up to increase your supply. Take good-sized tubers with 3 or more shoots; cut from top to bottom of the tuber, between the shoots, so each piece has a growing shoot. Dip cut surfaces in powdered charcoal or sulfur, and allow to dry for 3 or 4 days before starting them in a flat of sharp sand and peat moss.

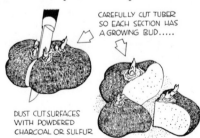

CAREFULLY CUT TUBER SO EACH SECTION HAS A GROWING BUD.....

DUST CUT SURFACES WITH POWDERED CHARCOAL OR SULFUR

SOFTWOOD CUTTINGS

The practice of rooting cuttings and raising them to mature flowering-sized plants is a rewarding one, assuring you of plants with the very same characteristics as the parent. (Seeds do not necessarily come true, and may yield plants differing greatly from the parent.) Here and on the next page, we show the steps in making and rooting softwood cuttings of common garden plants.

The terms softwood, semi-hard or greenwood, and hardwood refer to the maturity of the wood; softwood cuttings, which can be taken any time in spring during the active growing season, are the easiest and quickest rooting of the three types, and so are probably the best for the beginner to start with.

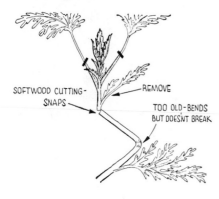

SOFTWOOD CUTTING SNAPS — REMOVE

TOO OLD-BENDS BUT DOESN'T BREAK

SELECTING CUTTING WOOD

Softwood cuttings can be taken from deciduous or evergreen shrubs or trees, or from herbaceous or evergreen perennials.

Lateral or side branches that have formed after the growing tip of the main stem of a plant has been pinched generally make good cuttings. Avoid abnormal growth: weak shoots from the center of the plant, or exceptionally vigorous, thick stems.

These plants are readily propagated from softwood cuttings:

Perennials and bulbs: Perennial alyssum, arabis, aubrieta, chrysanthemum, dahlia, delphinium, pelargonium, sedum, tuberous begonia.

Woody plants: Azalea, bougainvillea, ceanothus, daphne, gardenia, heather, hibiscus, honeysuckle, ivy, myrtus, oleander, plumbago, pyracantha, rose, star jasmine, wisteria.

MAKING CUTTINGS

See the photographs at right, on this page. Generally you should make the cut just below a leaf bud (node), but some plants will root just as well if you make the cut between nodes—an advantage if cutting wood is scarce. Among such plants are chrysanthemum, dahlia, fuchsia, big leaf hydrangea, penstemon, and lavender.

TAKE FUCHSIA CUTTINGS WHEN NEW SHOOTS ARE 2" TO 3" LONG

STRIP OFF LOWER LEAVES THAT MAY TOUCH ROOTING MEDIUM

If leaves are quite large, it may be necessary to cut back part of the leaf surface to lessen transpiration and to reduce the space required by the cutting in the propagating box. But where possible, retain as much of the foliage as you can.

PLANTING AND CARE OF CUTTINGS

You have a choice of good rooting mediums: coarse river sand; a mixture of half sand and half peat moss; half sand and half perlite; or vermiculite.

The sand and peat moss mix is best for acid loving plants such as azalea. Vermiculite has a tendency to stay quite moist, so use it with caution.

If you are rooting a large number of cuttings, a nursery flat makes a good propagating bed. For just a few, use a clay pan or one-pound coffee can.

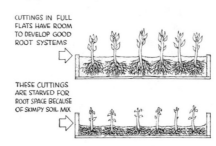

CUTTINGS IN FULL FLATS HAVE ROOM TO DEVELOP GOOD ROOT SYSTEMS

THESE CUTTINGS ARE STARVED FOR ROOT SPACE BECAUSE OF SKIMPY SOIL MIX

Bottom heat will speed up rooting. A soil temperature of 75° to 80° and an air temperature of 70° is ideal. You can generally expect softwood cuttings to root in two to five weeks.

DARROW M. WATT

1. *Early in the day, take 3 to 5-inch cuttings with at least two leaf buds. Keep in moist burlap or sphagnum moss in a cool place until you can plant them. Never soak or leave in sun.*

2. *Use pot label to level rooting medium before planting; firm afterward. Strip leaves off lower portion of cutting. Dip end in hormone powder to stimulate root growth. Water thoroughly.*

3. *Seal off container from outside air to keep soil moist, humidity high around cuttings. Here we use a piece of polyethylene film; inverted glass jar works as well (see photograph on next page).*

Step-by-step . . .

how to make an azalea cutting

DARROW M. WATT

1 • *Tip growth of current season—just mature enough to break when bent sharply—makes best cutting. Make a clean cut; remove flower buds if any.*

2 • *After stripping off lower leaves that would be buried, retain as much other foliage as possible. Make hole, insert cutting, firm it in well; water to settle.*

3 • *Glass jar, inverted in clay pot, makes good propagating case for azalea, daphne, or rose cutting. Raise jar occasionally to admit fresh air, keep mold from forming.*

DARROW M. WATT

4 • *Two or three months after planting, azalea's root system shows good development. Rooting mixture is half peat moss (moistened beforehand), half sand.*

HARDWOOD CUTTINGS

You can increase your supply of certain deciduous shrubs and trees by making hardwood cuttings in fall when plants are dormant, after leaves have fallen but before winter freezes come. Patience is the byword if you intend to propagate by this method, since most hardwood cuttings are slow in getting established (sometimes as long as a year).

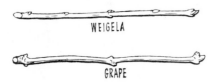

WEIGELA

GRAPE

Hardwood cuttings can be made of deutzia, forsythia, grapes, kolkwitzia, philadelphus, and weigela, to name just a few examples.

The following, however, do not root satisfactorily from hardwood cuttings and are normally propagated from seed, grafting, or budding: fruit trees, most nut trees, maple, oak, birch, linden, and beech trees.

CUTTING

Cut the tip of the branch back to where wood is about the size of a lead pencil. Make the cuttings 6 to 9 inches long; include at least two leaf nodes. Make the bottom cut a slanting one at, or just below, a node or leaf joint. Tie the cuttings of each variety together in a bundle, and attach a label marked with the name of the plant and date of cutting.

STORING

Dig a shallow trench in well drained soil. Put in the cuttings; cover them with about 2 inches of soil. In regions where the ground freezes, add enough mulch to keep the cuttings free from frosts.

You may, if you wish, store the cuttings in boxes of soil. If you do this, keep the

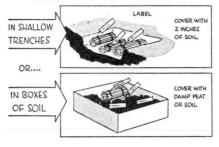

STORE HARDWOOD CUTTINGS

IN SHALLOW TRENCHES — LABEL — COVER WITH 2 INCHES OF SOIL

OR....

IN BOXES OF SOIL — COVER WITH DAMP PEAT OR SOIL

soil moist through the winter. Cuttings stored in the garden get enough moisture from the soil to keep their tissues from drying out.

By the time weather warms up in spring the cuttings will have formed calluses or roots, and they can be set in an open cutting bed.

ROOTING

Hardwood cuttings take a long time to root (sometimes as long as a year), and it is a good idea to start them in an out-of-the-way place while they grow to planting size. One good method is to bury a bottomless apple box halfway

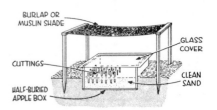

BURLAP OR MUSLIN SHADE
GLASS COVER
CUTTINGS
CLEAN SAND
HALF-BURIED APPLE BOX

in the ground and half fill it with clean sand. Insert the cuttings in the sand almost to their full length, and cover with a piece of glass. Above this, set a muslin or burlap covered frame (see sketch) to keep the sun's direct rays off the cuttings. Keep the planting medium damp but not waterlogged.

It is possible for gardeners in mild-winter areas to start hardwood cuttings outdoors in their permanent locations, immediately after taking them. There is little point to this, however, because root growth won't start for several months. (Remember that hardwood cuttings are taken during dormancy, whereas softwood cuttings are taken during the active growth period.)

ROOT AND LEAF CUTTINGS

ROOT CUTTINGS

Cuttings may be taken from the roots of any plant that produces sprouts from the roots. Actually, the roots you plant will show no visible buds; the buds develop after the root cutting is planted. Plants which may be propagated from root cuttings include: *Anemone Japonica,* Oriental poppy, trumpet creeper, plumbago, blackberry, and raspberry. To make root cuttings, select roots 3/16 to 3/8 inch in diameter from vigorous plants. Cut roots into pieces 1-3 inches long. Fill a box or flat to within about 1 inch of the top with light garden loam; place cuttings 2 inches apart in a horizontal position on top of the soil. Cover with about 1/2 inch of additional soil, and water thoroughly. Cover with glass or newspaper and place in the shade.

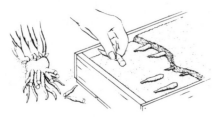

LEAF CUTTINGS

Under favorable conditions, even the leaves of certain plants will send out roots. Leaf cuttings are possible with fleshy-leafed plants, because a considerable amount of food is stored in the leaves. African violets, gloxinias, Rex begonias, and many succulents can be propagated this way.

Sometimes the entire leaf is used to propagate roots, in which case the petiole, or leaf stalk, is inserted in sand. In other cases the leaf is shortened, or cut into triangular sections. In the latter circumstance, leave a section of the petiole in each portion. Plant these pieces 1/2 inch deep in moist sand. Bottom heat helps to speed rooting.

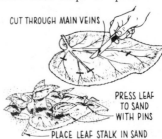

CUT THROUGH MAIN VEINS
PRESS LEAF TO SAND WITH PINS
PLACE LEAF STALK IN SAND

Rex begonia leaves will root if they are placed whole on top of moist sand, held down with toothpicks, kept moist, shaded and at constant temperature.

GRAFTING TECHNIQUES

On these pages we illustrate the wondrous and ancient horticultural practice called grafting—the operation of inserting a short piece of stem bearing one or more buds from one plant into another plant to form a union that grows together. If the graft succeeds, a branch grows from it and carries the flowers and fruits of the plant from which the piece of stem was taken; the rest of the plant will continue to carry its own flowers and fruits.

Many a home gardener has tried his hand at grafting, as much for the satis-faction of doing it and seeing the graft grow as for any practical purpose (such as adding another variety to a pear tree or to a camellia bush). It is a test of skill as well as a practical accomplishment.

Anyone interested in learning the art should first introduce two important words into his vocabulary: *stock* and *scion* (SIGH-un). Stock is the name for the plant onto which you graft. The scion is the piece of stem, containing one or more buds, that you insert in the stock.

It would be fun (for a while, perhaps) if you could graft a scion from any plant onto any other plant. But, nature doesn't allow that. Theoretically, for a graft to work, the scion and stock plants must be close botanical relations. But even that rule has its exceptions. We quote here a passage on the subject from *Grafting and Budding*, by W. P. Duruz, Oregon Extension Bulletin 528. "Experience finally determines the limits of grafting . . . For example, apples and pears are closely related, but they do not intergraft satisfactorily. Hawthorn and pear, which are somewhat more distantly related, can be grafted one to the other successfully. Pear can be grafted on quince, while the apple

---

Bark grafting . . . *best method for older trees, most successful for novices*

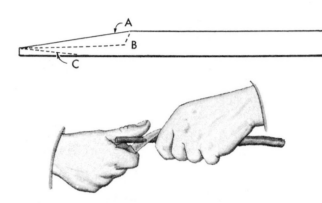

First, *make one slit like this for each scion. You can place 3 or 4 scions on the stock. Slice through bark to wood. Do bark grafting in early spring, when you can pull bark from wood. This means getting scions in winter and storing them in plastic bags in the refrigerator until spring.*

After slitting bark, *trim scions to fit. Leave 3 or 4 buds on each scion. Make a slanting slice on inner side (A). In addition, you can cut a ledge at top of inner slice (difficult cut) to fit over stock (B), and also taper outer side so scion can slide under one flap of the bark (C).*

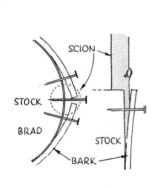

Lift bark *and insert scion under one flap or down the middle— whichever makes the snugger fit (scions trimmed as shown in example C, above, will fit best under one flap). Drive a wire brad through the bark and scion into stump. An extra: brads through flaps on each side of the scion.*

Immediately *after placing and nailing the scions, cover all cut surfaces with grafting wax or asphalt emulsion grafting compound. All scions may not grow. You probably wouldn't want to keep all, anyway. How to train and select the growing scions is shown in the illustrations on page 23.*

is seldom if ever propagated on the quince, and the quince does not grow well on either the apple or the pear.

"Apples are successfully grown only on apple stock, either standard or dwarf. The peach can be grown on the plum and vice versa. The apricot can be grafted on the peach, plum, or prune, but is not satisfactory on the almond. The sweet cherry can be grafted on the sour cherry, but will not graft onto any of the other stone fruits, even though they are closely related botanically."

Your safest first try at grafting probably would be to graft one variety of fruit (as apple or peach) onto another vari-ety of the same kind, or one variety of camellia onto another variety of camellia, wisteria onto wisteria, and so forth, until you become skilled. Then, try grafting from one plant onto another which you believe to be closely related.

The next word for a novice grafter to learn: *cambium*. It is the soft layer of tissue on a stem (or root) that lies between the bark and the wood. When you peel bark off a tree it comes loose at the cambium layer. Through cell division, this layer gives rise to new bark tissue on the outside and new wood tissue on the inside. In other words, it is the place from which growth on the mature part of a stem or branch origi-nates.

The crucial point of grafting is to align a section of the cambium layer of the

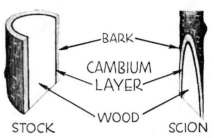

Cambium layers *of stock and scion must touch if graft is to be successful.*

Cleft grafting . . . *popular method but not ideal, has some notable faults*

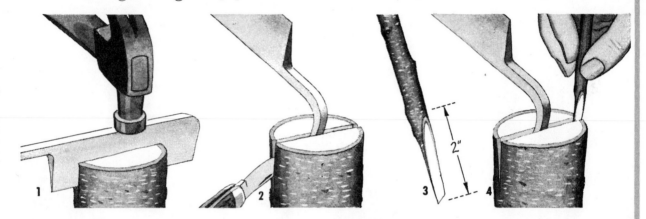

Experts criticize *this widely-used method because: allows only 2 or 4 scions; cleft split can go awry; rot can enter; cleft heals slowly; union can be weak. Use illustrated grafting tool, cleaver, or heavy knife. Illustrated procedure: (1) Lay graft-ing tool along the line to be cleft (where new branches should* grow), pound it in to make a cleft 6 inches deep. (2) Hammer in hook end (or wooden wedges) to hold cleft open. Trim sides smooth. (3) Trim scions to fit. (4) Insert the bigger scion first, making sure to place it so that the cambium layers of the scion and the stock line up with each other.*

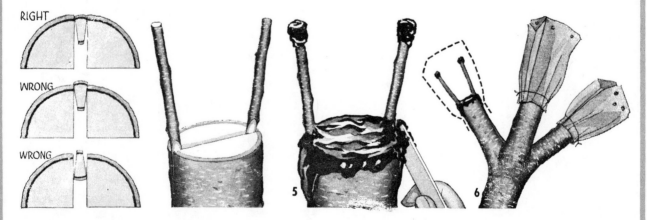

Pull hook out a bit to put pressure on bigger scion before inserting smaller one. Figures at left look down at cleft graft, show right and wrong positions for scions (wrong positions do not bring cambium layers into contact). Be sure to leave ½ inch of cut surface on scions exposed above surface of stock (makes stronger union). (5) After removing grafting tool or wedges, cover cut surfaces with grafting wax. (6) If weather is very cold or dry before grafts are well started, cover with paper bags, punctured for air. Be sure to remove the bags if the temperature goes above 85°.*

scion with the cambium layer of the stock, as completely as possible, and then bind the stock and scion together so that a union takes place between the two cambiums. A graft can succeed only if you line up the cambium layers—in some places, if not completely.

The knives that you use should be high-quality steel, kept very sharp. A sharp tool makes a clean slice, thereby insuring maximum contact of cambium layers.

There's a way to cut scions without cutting yourself: Sit down and hold scion horizontally against your chest, with end to be cut at your right (left if you're left-handed). Hold knife as shown in bark grafting sequence. Pull to right to make cuts, *moving thumb with knife*. You may court trouble if you slide knife in front of a thumb held rigidly.

All grafting methods shown here, except one, call for sawing branch or trunk back to a stub. Cut the stub cleanly and smoothly. If the branch is heavy or horizontal, pre-cut as shown below, left.

Final cut *must be smooth, no torn bark.*

In all grafting methods, the tight union between stock and scion must be sealed off from air with some kind of sealing agent. Probably easiest for a novice is ready made tree sealing compound (water base asphalt emulsion) that comes in cans. If it rains during first 24 hours after applying, examine for wash-off; you may need to apply more.

Graft deciduous trees and shrubs any time during the dormant season. Usually it's most satisfactory if done before buds begin to swell in late winter or early spring. Evergreens can be grafted in early spring, just before plants begin to grow actively.

Saw kerf grafting . . . *beginners find it difficult, experts like it best*

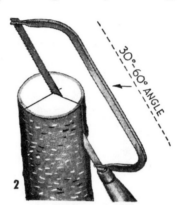

First of all, cut the scion (outer side shown at left, inner side at right). (2) Draw guide lines with a pencil. With fine-toothed saw, cut straight into trunk (not at oblique angle), twice as far down as across the top. (3) Hold inner side of scion against the saw cut (kerf). With knife, bevel kerf sides to fit scion using bottom ⅓ of scion's cut portion for pattern. (4) Using a stick for a mallet, gently tap scion into kerf, matching cambiums and leaving ¼ inch of the cut scion sur-

face showing above the stock. If scion wiggles at the bottom, bevel more from the kerf's top, and vice versa. Seal and cover, (5) and (6), as for cleft (page 21). Advantages of saw kerf grafting: you can do it on a limb too large, too knotty, or too twisted for a cleft; makes a strong union during first year; you can use 3 or more scions where you want them (the cleft is usually limited to 2 in opposing positions) and even if you keep only 1 or 2 of them, the others help heal.

Side grafting . . . *useful for adding a branch on the side of a tree*

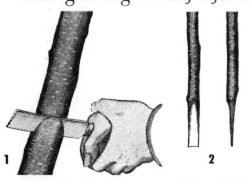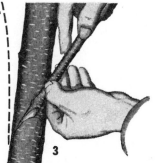

Use this method *on branches too small for bark, cleft, or saw kerf grafting, and too large for wedge or whip graft. It's a way to add a branch where none grows. You don't remove top of stock. (1) Make an oblique-angled slice into stock. (2) Cut wedge-shaped scion, slanting sides slightly longer* than length of cut into stock, longer cut on inner side of scion than on outer side. Lowest bud should face out. (3) Bend stock to open cut. Insert the scion so that the cambium layers meet on one side. (4) Tie the graft if springback of branch doesn't hold it. Wax the cut surfaces.*

Whip and wedge grafting . . . *ways to graft small scions on small stocks*

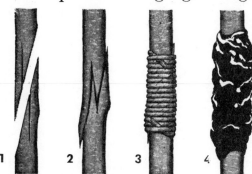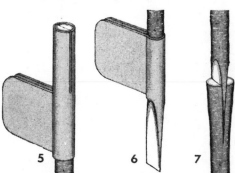

Figures (1) through (4) *show steps in making whip graft. (1) Make slanting, through-cuts on stock and scion. Make second cuts into each, starting about 1/3 distance from opposite tips, cutting almost parallel to original cut. (2) Fit scion. (3) Wrap or tape tightly. (4) Cover with wax.*

Wedge grafting, *another method for small stocks and scions, here using patented set of manufactured templates or pattern shields. (5) With one pattern you cut cleft into stock. (6) With matching scion pattern, cut as scion or wedge to fit. (7) Insert scion. (8) Wrap and wax.*

After the graft grows . . . *the important business of selecting and training*

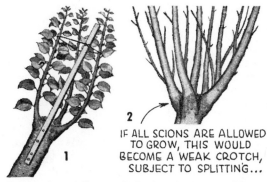

2 — IF ALL SCIONS ARE ALLOWED TO GROW, THIS WOULD BECOME A WEAK CROTCH, SUBJECT TO SPLITTING...

3 — SO INSTEAD, TRAIN TO ONE DOMINANT BRANCH, DISCOURAGE ALL THE OTHERS...

4 — DISCOURAGE BY PRUNING BACK UNWANTED BRANCHES AT END OF 1st YEAR, LEAVE SELECTED BRANCH ALONE

5 — CUT ON DOTTED LINE. IF ONLY ONE SCION GROWS, SLICE OFF DEAD SHOULDER ON OPPOSITE SIDE OF STOCK

Frequently, *until growth begins, inspect grafting wax for splits; rewax any that develop. Optional: In hot areas, whitewash the entire grafted tree, including grafts, to protect from sunburn. (1) Tie or tack 1 by 2-inch strips of lath to the stock as support for bark grafts and others that are not well* anchored. (2) This is why you shouldn't leave all scions. (3) How one grafted branch should take over. Subdued branches have a function—they help to heal the graft. (4) How to encourage one branch, subdue others. (5) Remove the dead shoulder on stock here if only one scion takes.*

BUDDING: T- bud

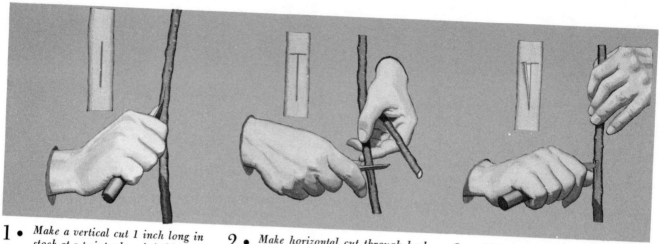

1 • *Make a vertical cut 1 inch long in stock at a point where it is ¼ to ½ inch in diameter. Slice to the wood.*

2 • *Make horizontal cut through bark across top of the vertical cut, about. 1/3 the distance around the stock.*

3 • *Lift corners. If bark sticks tight or breaks, don't bud now—plant is too dry or it's too late in season.*

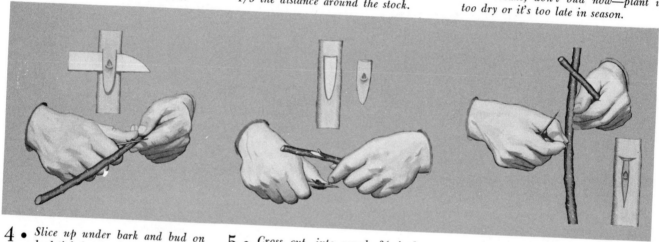

4 • *Slice up under bark and bud on budstick (see text). Make slice from ½ inch below to 1 inch above bud.*

5 • *Cross cut, into wood, ¾ inches above bud. Push shield out sidewise. Wood core in bud should stay.*

6 • *Push shield downward under loosened flaps of bark in T until top cuts on shield and stock are even.*

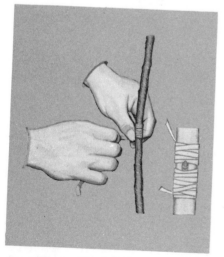

7 • *Wrap with plastic or rubber strip. Cover strip's top with first full wrap; insert end under last wrap.*

In summer and early fall comes the season for the kind of propagating that professionals call "summer budding."

You insert a bud from one plant under the bark of a plant of a related variety. If the two varieties are compatible and if you are skillful (or lucky), the bud and the plant will unite. Through the fall and winter, the live, plump bud remains dormant. In spring, when the surge of growth comes to all the buds on the plant, the implanted bud also starts to grow and you cut back to just above it.

All the growth from the implanted bud —flowers, fruits, and leaves—will have the characteristics of the plant from which you took the bud.

You have nothing to lose in experimenting with this technique; if the bud fails, the tree or shrub is not harmed.

(A *graft* that doesn't take, on the other hand, disfigures the plant.) You stand to gain in two ways: You get the journeyman's satisfaction that comes with mastering a new skill; and you can convert a plant to a better variety or add another variety to an existing plant, for novelty or for some practical purpose such as furnishing a pollinating variety within a fruit tree's structure. Nurserymen use summer budding to convert easily grown seedling bushes or tree saplings to varieties that people want but that cannot be grown easily from seed. They place the bud in the bottom 3 or 4 inches of the seedling.

The plant and the section of branch into which you place the bud is called the *stock*. The buds come from the *budstick*, a length of branch containing several buds which you cut from the

BUDDING: Patch-bud

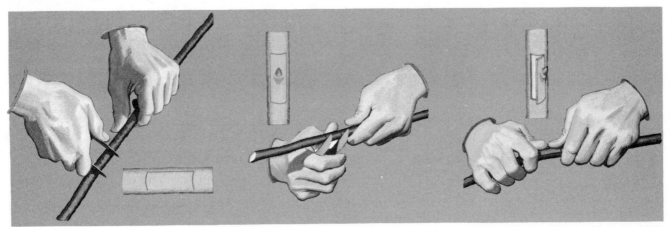

1 • *With tool, make parallel cuts 1/3 distance around stock, and one vertical cut, forming a square C.*

2 • *On budstick, make parallel cuts above and below bud, vertical connecting cuts on each side of bud.*

3 • *Press bud patch out from budstick with sideway pressure, so that the core of wood will remain in the bud.*

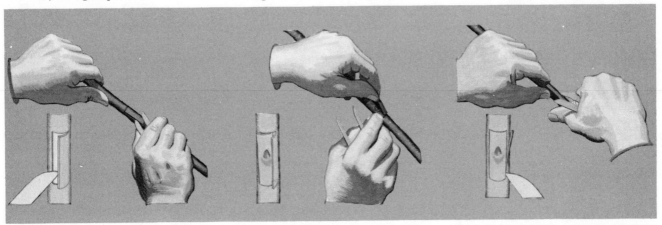

4 • *On stock, lift vertical edge of square C made in step 1. The bud patch will slide under this flap.*

5 • *Slide bud patch under lifted flap until patch sits flat on bare wood. Trim overhang on flap and patch.*

6 • *If bud patch is thinner than bark on stock, pare bark on the stock so tying will hold the patch tight.*

introduced variety. It should not differ greatly in size from the section of stock, and it should be fresh. Also, it should bear vegetative buds, not flowering buds.

To implant a bud into the upper branches of a big tree or older bush, choose a branch of one to two-year-old wood, remove foliage that would interfere with the budding operation, and proceed as shown in either of the two methods above.

Usually, you will find the buds on the budstick at the base of leaf stalks. Remove the leaf, but don't cut off the leaf stalk. Use it as a handle and also as an indicator: If, when it withers a week or two after budding, the bud remains plump and green, then the operation is a success. But if the entire bud shield or patch (bark, bud, and leaf stalk)

withers or turns dark, the operation has failed.

In a few weeks cut off the tying material if it appears to be constricting the stock. Late the following winter, cut off the old stock above the bud and it will grow into a flourishing stem.

The T-bud method illustrated on page 24 is the easiest one for a novice, and is the most widely used. Use patch budding, shown on this page, with plants that have thick bark, such as walnuts, pecans, and avocados. Double-bladed tools for patch budding, shown in the sequence above, are manufactured but are not widely sold. You can make one with two knife blades mounted on a block so that they will be 1¼ inches apart. Knives for any kind of budding should be kept very sharp. Both methods work only if bark pulls away from the wood easily.

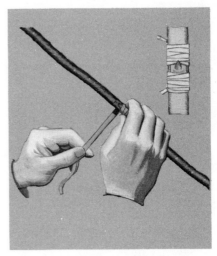

7 • *Tie as for T-bud. Or, you can secure this kind of bud with gummed paper tape or polyethylene tape.*

LAYERING

Layering is a simple method of plant propagation in which branches are notched and brought into contact with the soil to make them take root while still attached to the parent plant. Later they can be detached to become new plants.

By using this technique, it's possible to propagate plants that are not easily rooted from cuttings, such as magnolias, pieris, and rhododendrons. You can increase your stock of vines, shrubs, perennials, and even some small trees this way. Azalea, rhododendron, daphne, forsythia, tree peony, cotoneaster, rosemary, dianthus, sarcococca, juniper, and penstemon layer quite easily.

Layering is a more convenient way to start a few new plants than rooting of cuttings.

New plants you get from layering should be transplanted in late fall if you live in a mild climate; if your winters are cold, wait until spring. Keep slow rooting shrubs, like rhododendrons, in place for another full year to permit the development of a sturdy root system. You can leave perennials in place and transplant when the weather cools in fall.

Early spring is the preferred time for layering woody plants, although layers made in fall or winter are also successful, as a rule. Ivy, star jasmine, ceanothus, junipers, and several other ground covers will spread much faster if you make several layers along each branch without separating it from the parent plant. (They spread like strawberry plants.)

1 • *Select a vigorous, young branch growing close to ground or one flexible enough to bend. Mark a point about 12 inches from end of branch just below a node; directly below, make a 4-inch-deep hole. Mix soil with equal parts peat moss or ground bark, sand.*

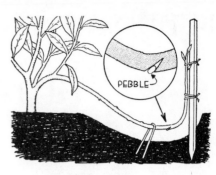

2 • *On underside of branch at marked point, make slanting cut half way through; wedge in pebble. Bend branch into hole; anchor it to soil with heavy wire loop. Bring end of branch to vertical position; stake. Fill hole with prepared soil, firm; then water thoroughly.*

3 • *Place a brick or stone on the soil directly above layered stem section; this will keep the soil firm and help to hold the moisture. In cold winter areas, you should also spread a mulch of leaves over the layer to protect it, leaving tip and several of the leaves exposed.*

4 • *Check to see if the layer has rooted (it will take from 9 months to a year for woody plants, about 6 weeks for perennials) by carefully removing the soil on top of the layer. When roots are well established, sever stem from parent plant just below the original cut.*

AIR LAYERING

Air layering is an ancient, well proven, and highly interesting technique. It is an excellent method for increasing choice shrubs and trees, as it often works on plants which are difficult or impossible to root by other methods. Polyethylene plastic material makes the process quite simple. Here's how:

Select a branch from a pencil size up to an inch in diameter. Below a node either make a slanting cut 1/3 through the stem, inserting a piece of matchstick to keep it spread apart, or remove a ring of bark about 3/4 inch wide,

scraping it clean down to the heartwood.

Dust the cut lightly with hormone powder, wrap the area with a generous handful of damp sphagnum, and tie it up in polyethylene. Bind it securely above and below the cut with string or wire ties.

This procedure is well worth trying on choice plants such as deciduous magnolias. Philodendrons also take well to this process. If it works, you'll see roots appearing in the sphagnum moss in a month or two. Then you can separate the youngster from the mother plant. If it doesn't root, the branch will

callus, new bark will eventually grow over the cut area, and you're no worse off than before.

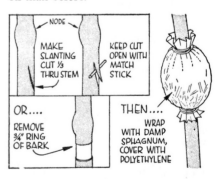

Roots develop *in the moist sphagnum.*

CHAPTER 3

Planting Procedures

ERNEST BRAUN

PLANTING FROM FLATS

The story behind a sunny border of summer annuals in full bloom is told in the photographs on these three pages.

To anyone who has gardened a long time, these basic steps will be familiar; some veterans may even differ with us on a few details. But there's no need to debate fine points: The important principle, on which all gardeners agree, is that a planting job well done from beginning to end is rewarding both in what it does for the plants and in the satisfaction it brings the gardener.

WHEN IS IT TIME TO DIG AND PLANT?

In mild climates, April and May are favored months both for preparing the soil and setting out transplants of many kinds of summer annuals.

In sections where late spring frosts are likely, ready your borders for planting as soon as you can work the ground— the time-honored test is met when you can crumble the soil to a fine texture in your hand, or break it up easily with a fork or spade. If you have a light, sandy soil, any fine day is a good time to get out and dig. But beware of digging a heavy clay soil when it is wet; each spadeful of soggy earth will turn into a big clod that will be practically impossible to pulverize after it has become hard and dry.

Ideal temperatures at planting time should be something like this: daytime ground temperatures averaging about 50°; daytime air temperatures ranging between 60° and 80°; nighttime air temperatures between 40° and 50°.

There would be little point in setting out marigolds (shown here) early while the weather is still cold; they would simply stand still until activated by favorable temperatures. A sudden freeze could, of course, kill them. The same applies to all summer annuals and warm weather vegetables.

WEEDING, WATERING, PINCHING, FEEDING, SHADING

The photographs here show the planting process only. There are other important preliminary and follow-through steps that can undo all your careful work unless you heed them:

Weeding. Hoe off weeds before you dig. Don't turn them under if you expect to set out plants within a few weeks; it takes a long time for buried weeds to break down.

Watering. Newly set out plants need frequent watering. Once they are well established, let the weather and your soil conditions determine how often to water. Test the soil; when it dries to an inch or two below the surface, water thoroughly.

Pinching. A week or two after setting out transplants, pinch them back to encourage branching and heavier flower production. Annuals such as balsam, dianthus, petunia, and phlox benefit from pinching of the growing tips throughout the summer.

Feeding. About a month after setting out plants, boost them by feeding with a complete fertilizer. Discontinue feeding after plants start to bloom.

Shading. Plants transferred from a cool lathhouse into full sun need protection in case of a sudden hot spell. If this should occur, shade them with lath frames, shingles, cardboard, newspapers, or plastic shade cloth.

DARROW M. WATT

1 • *Push fork straight down to full depth. Turn under any of the various humus-building materials (soil amendments are discussed on pages 4 and 5). Work backward.*

4 • *To facilitate removal of first row of plants, jar one end of flat sharply against ground. Entire soil mass will shift to lower end. Flat should be watered day before planting.*

2 . *Lift forkful of soil, turn over to reverse top and lower levels of soil. Break clods. Pile each forkful slightly forward; "trench" just ahead of feet fills as you dig.*

3 . *Rake surface, small section at a time, to maintain constant level and to avoid trampling after digging. Remove rocks and any hard clods you can't break down with rake.*

5 . *With putty knife or spatula, block out plants by cutting straight down around each one. Another good method is to carefully tear each plant out so roots remain intact.*

6 . *With plant removed from flat, root-filled block of soil looks somewhat like a piece of chocolate cake. A plant treated like this rarely suffers transplant shock.*

(continued on next page)

7 • *Dig generous holes with straight sides, large enough to accommodate root ball without squeezing it in. Provide ample space for backfilling hole with loose, fine soil.*

8 • *Firm soil around root ball with fingers. Set plant so top of root ball is slightly lower than it was in the flat. Form a small basin around the plant for watering.*

DARROW M. WATT

9 • *Mulch with humous material—peat moss, ground bark, sawdust, leaf mold, or rotted manure—to conserve soil moisture, prevent surface caking, inhibit weed growth.*

10 • *About 10 weeks after setting out, marigolds planted according to directions were in full bloom. In hot, dry climates, dwarf and tall zinnias are a better choice.*

BALLED & BURLAPPED SHRUBS AND TREES

Balled and burlapped plants (often referred to as B & B) are widely available in many sections of the country. Growers dig plants in summer and early fall, wrap the root balls in burlap, and ship them to nurseries in time for the proper planting season. Many evergreens are sold B & B, as are certain large deciduous trees.

1. *Burlap and twine are all that hold root ball together, so handle with care. Burlap should be taut, tied securely, with no part of the root ball exposed.*

2. *When bringing plants home, make sure they won't roll around. You may have to prop trunks. A well tied root ball is least likely to be damaged.*

3. *Don't use trunk as a handle. If ball isn't tight, it will loosen even more. Be careful not to hit the ball against something while you are carrying it.*

4. *If plant isn't too heavy, cradle the root ball in your arms, with one hand supporting the bottom. Plants are easier to handle if you bind the branches.*

5. *Two can carry fairly heavy plants in sling of canvas, burlap, or any strong fabric (don't use old or rotted material). Support the stem or trunk.*

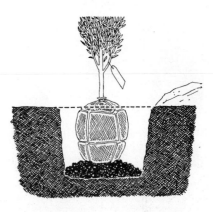

6. *Planting hole should be about twice width of root ball. Set plant on cushion of loose soil mix so top of the ball is slightly higher than surrounding ground.*

7. *Most plants have a "best side," so before you fill in the hole it's a good idea to untie branches, rotate the plant until it faces in right direction.*

8. *Fill hole about half full with prepared soil mix, firming with stick. If supporting stake is needed, put it in now so that you don't damage the root ball.*

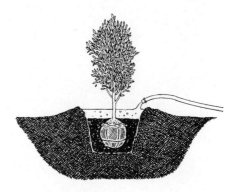

9. *Loosen twine and burlap at top of ball; fill hole to top with soil. Build water basin by hoeing up circle of soil. Soak well, filling the basin two or three times.*

PLANTING BARE-ROOT

Many kinds of deciduous trees and shrubs are sold bare-root during winter and early spring. This is a popular method of planting; nurseries offer a wide selection at this time, and you'll pay less money than if you wait to buy the same plants in containers months later.

It is a good idea to dig your planting hole and prepare some soil mix before you get the tree home. This means you can plant immediately, without having to keep the roots moist while you're working. If you must delay planting, for weather or other reasons, keep the roots well covered with wet burlap. Or, set the roots loosely in a temporary trench (see sketch).

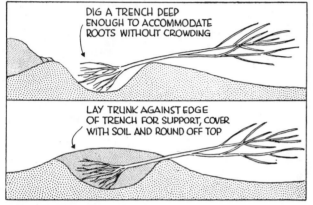

If plants arrive *from a supplier while the ground is frozen, put them in a trench like this until weather warms. You could also keep them in a box of wet sawdust or peat moss.*

If you receive a plant with dry roots, stand it in water for a few hours. Roses suffer especially if roots are dry.

You can dig a planting hole that's only slightly larger than the plant's root system, but you're far ahead of the game if you dig a good-sized hole and use a "transition zone" soil

mix, described and pictured at the bottom of this page. Check drainage before you plant. Fill the planting hole with water and see how long it takes to drain away. If the soil is dry, it may take less than an hour to disappear; if it's wet soil, it may take several hours. If the water just stands in the hole, check for hardpan or change location to a higher spot. Drainage and hardpan are discussed on pages 6 and 7.

Drive in the supporting stake *before* you plant. If you wait until afterwards, you may damage the roots.

When you form the planting mound in the bottom of the hole, firm it with your hands; then spread the tree roots evenly over the mound. Trim off any bruised or broken roots with a sharp knife or pruning shears.

Bare-root planting can be extremely difficult if you do it all by yourself. Get an assistant to help steady the tree (you can coax him into it by telling him, in all honesty, that he won't have to work very hard!)

Two important follow-through steps can, if neglected, spoil the future of even the most carefully planted tree or shrub:

1. If the tree came with a name label, be sure the wire holding the name label isn't too tight. Move the label from the main trunk to a smaller side branch. We've seen trees choked to death by wire that cut into the trunk as the tree grew.

2. Build up a water-holding ridge of soil around the tree; then *extend* this water basin each year to just beyond the dripline (extremity of branches), so spreading feeder roots will continue to get water as the tree grows.

The bare-root planting season varies, depending on your climate. Mild-climate gardeners plant in winter; in cold-winter regions, the season begins as soon as the ground thaws in spring. Wherever you live, you'll know the season is about over when spring weather begins to warm up. The earlier you get them in, the better; if you wait until a bare-root plant begins to put on leaves, it may suffer a setback in planting—you might even lose it.

Follow these 10 steps to plant a young tree or shrub:

In the sketches on the right you see the ideal soil picture for planting bare-root trees. "Transition zone" soil contains approximately 1 part of organic material and 3 parts of native soil. A loosened, enriched soil mixture of this type encourages roots to grow out of the root zone into the surrounding native soil.

To get "root zone" soil, mix native soil from the hole with an equal amount of organic material such as peat moss.

This general planting procedure applies to both trees and bare-root shrubs; however, with shrubs a smaller stake is sufficient. Remove the stake from shrubs by the end of the first growing season. Keep trees staked for 2 or 3 years.

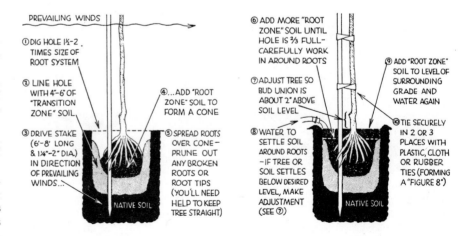

To make sure *water gets down deep, build a watering basin around plant, soak with hose.*

GROWING BULBS IN OPEN GROUND

Most spring blooming bulbs perform well with a minimum of care. However, if you expect maximum performance and beautiful blooms year after year, it is important that bulbs be given a good start.

The first step in open-ground planting is to dig the soil at least 12 to 18 inches deep. If you have a rich, easily worked soil, nothing need be added except perhaps some bonemeal, as shown here. But if your soil is poor or heavy, add humus in the form of leaf mold, peat moss, or finely ground bark. If you use manure, be sure it is well rotted—*never fresh*—and dig it in well below the depth at which you will set the bulbs, so that it will not come in contact with them.

Whether you plant one bulb to a hole or several at one time, be sure to plant all bulbs at a uniform depth, so they will bloom at the same time.

Single bulb planting. *First, dig hole in thoroughly prepared soil. Depth will vary according to size of bulb—usually about 3 times its greatest diameter. Work a tablespoon of bonemeal into soil in bottom of hole. Next place a 1-inch layer of sand on top. Then set the bulb and cover it with soil.*

Multiple bulb planting. *Excavate trench to required depth— 3 times greatest diameter of bulbs. Lightly cover bottom of trench with bonemeal and mix with soil. Apply 1-inch layer of sand over bottom of trench. Set large bulbs 5 to 6 inches apart, smaller bulbs 2 to 4 inches apart. Fill trench with soil.*

How deep do you plant?

Charted below are planting depths for various kinds of spring flowering bulbs that should be planted in the fall. In loamy soil, plant roughly 2½ to 3 times the greatest diameter of the bulb, excluding the neck; in heavy soil, plant less deeply. Bulbs set out later than November should also be planted less deeply, for they will have less time in which to push growth to the surface.

DARROW M. WATT

Bulb cover plants. *To avoid planting directly on top of bulbs, mark position of each bulb with small pile of sand. Set plants in spaces between, then soak bed thoroughly with fine spray. Pansies (shown here) or violas are good choices. Or sow seeds of shallow-rooted annuals, such as alyssum, directly over the bed.*

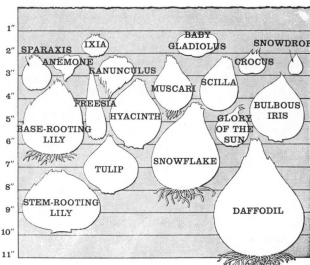

PLANTING FROM CANS

Planting from cans is popular with millions of gardeners—particularly in California and other mild-climate areas.

If you buy plants in cans or other containers, a healthy root system is of prime importance. It is difficult, of course, to know how healthy a specimen you are getting, since you cannot see the roots. Even a fairly healthy appearing plant may have roots that are: 1) underdeveloped, or 2) rootbound from being kept in the same can too long. You won't have to worry about such pitfalls if you follow this important advice: *Buy from a reliable nursery.*

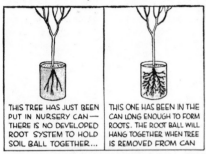

THIS TREE HAS JUST BEEN PUT IN NURSERY CAN—THERE IS NO DEVELOPED ROOT SYSTEM TO HOLD SOIL BALL TOGETHER...

THIS ONE HAS BEEN IN THE CAN LONG ENOUGH TO FORM ROOTS. THE ROOT BALL WILL HANG TOGETHER WHEN TREE IS REMOVED FROM CAN

When buying *a deciduous plant, ask if the roots are fully developed. If they aren't, keep the plant in the can for a month or so before planting.*

THIS CAMELLIA HAS 6 BUDS—IS FORCED-LOOKING, SPINDLY, WITH POOR STRUCTURE

NO BUDS, BUT IT'S A MUCH BETTER PLANT—LOW BRANCHING MEANS GOOD FORM WILL FOLLOW

Choose *plants for form, not for the number of flowers or berries they have.*

When setting out plants from cans, follow the procedures shown in the sketches (right). Steps 6 through 9 in the B & B planting process on page 31 show a very similar method that is equally recommended for canned plants.

Best time to cut the can is just before you plant. If the cans have already been cut by your nurseryman and you must delay planting for weather or other reasons, put them in a protected location and water occasionally to keep roots moist.

HARD ROOT FILLED BALL

LOOSEN ROOTS IN BOTTOM OF HARD ROOT BALL WITH POINTED STICK OR KNIFE

If roots *are so crowded that you can't break them out of the root ball, the plant will have trouble, may not survive.*

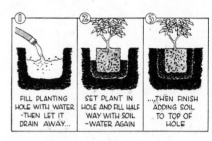

① FILL PLANTING HOLE WITH WATER—THEN LET IT DRAIN AWAY...

② SET PLANT IN HOLE AND FILL HALF WAY WITH SOIL—WATER AGAIN

③ ...THEN FINISH ADDING SOIL TO TOP OF HOLE

Water again *after adding last of soil mix; build water basin around plant.*

Many nurseries sell plants in tarpaper pots rather than cans. They are safe to handle and easy to dispose of. The sides of the pots can be slit very easily with a knife, but be careful not to dig it into the root ball as you cut.

How to carry, cut, and kick cans . . .

Handling plants in cans with know-how can save you time, trouble, and a few cuts (notice the gloves). Here we show ways to carry cans, as well as procedures for cutting and disposing of them.

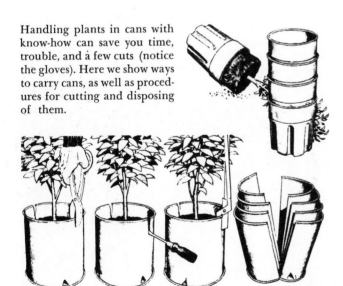

Cut cans *with tin shears, notched screwdriver, or manufactured cutter. Make 2 cuts, on opposite sides.* **Top right:** *crimped gallon cans need no cutting, nest easily.* **Lower right:** *nest cut cans for disposal. Be careful of sharp edges.*

MAKE A GRIP INTO THE SIDE OF BIG CANS

At top, *ways to carry two gallon can plants in each hand: index finger in the middle (left); manufactured device like pliers (right).* **Below:** *Heavier cans can be kicked to make a grip, then carried one at a time or one in each hand.*

FROM CAN TO TUB...
...STEP-BY-STEP

Potting up a canned shrub or small tree is really quite a simple procedure, as you can see from these photographs. Here are three additional tips:

1. What kind of soil mix you use depends to a large extent on the plant and the characteristics of your local soil which you may wish to include in the mix. Don't guess—ask your nurseryman what he recommends.

2. Don't choose a container that is too large or too small for the plant. Plants will need some root room, but don't give them too much.

3. Be sure the container has drainage holes in the bottom.

3. Remove loose soil around roots. Place a few small pieces from a broken pot around drainage hole to keep it from becoming clogged with soil. Add some soil mix.

1. Shrub ready to be transplanted into tub. Can sits on piece of heavy paper that will make the clean-up job easier. Sketches on facing page shows ways to cut a can.

4. Set plant in container; fill with soil mix to 2 inches from top. This mix (for camellia) is 1 part soil, 1 part peat moss, 1 part fine sand, and 2 parts oak leaf mold.

2. After cutting each side, lay can on its side. On large can such as this, cut bead at the bottom on both sides so that the can will pull apart easily. Be careful not to damage foliage.

HERBERT V. MITCHELL

5. When you have finished, water to wet new soil, settle plant in container. Add about an inch of mulch to help keep surface roots cool and to retain moisture in soil.

RE-POTTING TECHNIQUES

Sooner or later the roots of a plant in a container will fill all available space, and the plant becomes rootbound. Growth slows down or stops completely as the roots become coiled or twined, and even with a stepped-up watering and feeding program the plant will lose vigor and may eventually die. Therefore, if you suspect a rootbound condition, you should remove the plant from its container and have a look at the root ball. (Actually, if you have small plants on which you are trying to speed growth, you should move them into large pots never allowing them to become potbound.)

Re-potting large shrubs and trees in heavy containers is not so easy as when you are dealing with small plants, but you can rejuvenate them by root pruning and replanting them in some fresh soil.

The sketches on these two pages show you how to handle both the little ones and the big ones.

To get plants out of small pots . . .

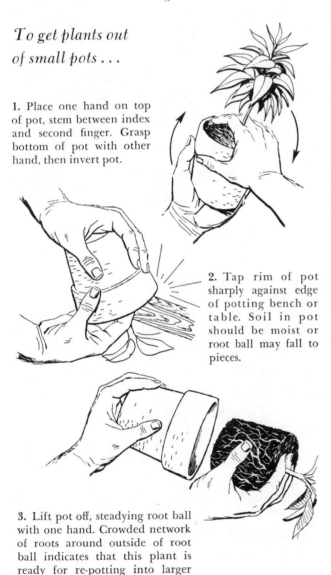

1. Place one hand on top of pot, stem between index and second finger. Grasp bottom of pot with other hand, then invert pot.

2. Tap rim of pot sharply against edge of potting bench or table. Soil in pot should be moist or root ball may fall to pieces.

3. Lift pot off, steadying root ball with one hand. Crowded network of roots around outside of root ball indicates that this plant is ready for re-potting into larger quarters.

Moving small plants into larger quarters . . .

1. Move plant into pot one size larger; for fast growers you can skip a size. Use clean pots and soak them in water first, especially if they are new. Cut off any roots that twine around the root ball.

2. Score root ball with knife, making ⅛ to ¼-inch-deep cuts. 3. Put concave piece of crock over drain hole; fill around it with gravel. Put in cushion of new soil to bring top of root ball 1 inch below rim of new pot. Fill in with soil, firm with stick.

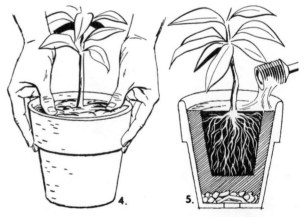

4. Add more soil, then firm around edges with your thumbs. 5. Water thoroughly so both new soil and soil in root ball are wet. As an added precaution, drench plant and soil with an all-purpose insecticide. It's a good idea to set plants in the shade for a few days.

Removing from large pots or containers ...

If possible, grow large plants in containers that can be taken apart easily when it comes time to root prune plants or when you want to transplant them into the ground.

Have at least one side that's removable so you can slide out the heavy root ball.

Otherwise let soil dry out slightly so ball slides out more easily, lay container on side, tap around rim with mallet or hammer while you (or a helper) pull gently but steadily on the trunk. Protect rim of the container with cloth.

You can also "float" out the root ball of some plants by forcing water through the drain hole in the bottom. Be sure to hold hose nozzle tightly against hole.

Root pruning, returning to original containers

1. After you remove the plant from its container, shave off a few inches of the root ball with a sharp knife (as little as 1 inch on small plants; 4 or 5 inches on large ones). This removes old soil and helps prune roots. Unwind and cut off large roots that encircle outside of root ball. Scoring the root ball with a knife will also cut most of these twining roots.

2. Put 1 or 2 inches of crushed rock, broken pots, or gravel, in bottom of container for drainage. Put in cushion of new soil (usually a little more than was shaved off the bottom). Replace plant. Top of root ball should be 2 inches below rim of container for watering.

3. Fill in around root ball with fresh soil mix. Work it into crevice between the root ball and container sides with a stick or length of metal reinforcing rod. Since containers are heavy, try to replant where the container is to remain. But if you don't, at least move it into location before you water.

4. The final step is to soak with water until both the new soil *and* the root ball are thoroughly saturated. You may have to fill the container to the rim three or four times. Let water run slowly. If there is some settling, add more soil. Repeat entire process when roots once again fill the container.

MOVING A SHRUB OR SMALL TREE

In many ways, a shrub or tree is to a garden what a chair or couch is to a living room: a basic fixture. Nevertheless, you may have to move it some time.

There can be several good reasons for transplanting a shrub to a new location. Frequently, new buildings or growing trees may cast shade on a plant which, up until then, was thriving in a sunny location. Or the opposite: down comes a fence, wall, or tree, and a shade-loving shrub suddenly finds itself struggling in a hot, sunny environment.

Perhaps you have just moved into a house with an established garden that doesn't jibe with your own landscaping tastes. Or perhaps you want to fumigate the soil in a disease-infested garden bed, which will require digging plants for replanting later on when the chemicals have done their work and the soil is once again safe for plant roots.

Have planting holes ready before lifting a plant in the garden or bringing one home from the nursery. (Planting procedure is described on page 31.) Never set the plant deeper than it was in its previous location.

It pays to know the eventual size of whatever you plant or transplant so you can allow plenty of space for it to mature naturally. Set all plants, including vines, at least a foot from a wall or fence.

Plants out of the ground should not be allowed to dry out or freeze. Transplant the same day if possible; otherwise, keep them in a shady, wind-protected place and plant when the first good opportunity arises.

It is a good idea to protect newly planted evergreens with a screen to prevent sun scorch, particularly if you transplant during hot weather (see page 76).

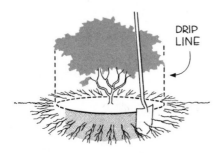

1. *(Optional.) Cut outer roots several weeks before transplanting. Shrub can adjust to minor shock, will form fresh feeder roots closer to main stem.*

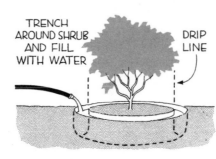

2. *Soak roots like this 2 or 3 days before moving plant. The water will penetrate into the root area and help hold the soil in a firm ball for easier handling.*

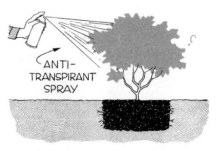

3. *(Optional.) A coating of anti-transpirant spray slows down loss of water through plant foliage. Available in pressure cans at many nurseries.*

4. *Decide on size of root ball which will sever fewest roots; cut down with spade or back of shovel. Heavy soil will allow larger root ball than sandy soil.*

5. *Cut down sides of hole to make room for undercutting and wrapping. Cut half way under root ball on one side. Be careful not to crumble root ball.*

6. *Wrap burlap sacking around ball as tightly as possible. Pin the burlap together with large nails; roll it underneath the cut half of the root ball.*

7. *Undercut the other side. Care must be taken not to break ball at this stage. Lift plant using shovel as lever; steady plant with free hand as you lift.*

8. *Place plant on open sack beside hole. Tip ball slightly, remove shovel. Plant is now ready for final wrapping with burlap. Fold the sack up to the trunk.*

9. *Wrap with heavy twine, starting at base of plant; wrap upward to secure entire ball. Tie frequently to prevent slipping when plant is moved.*

TRANSPLANTING BULBS AND PERENNIALS

IF YOU CAN'T DIVIDE AND REPLANT PERENNIALS THE SAME DAY, COVER WITH MOIST BURLAP OR SET ON SHEET OF POLYETHYLENE OR VINYL

BULBS

Remember that a bulb takes its first important step toward next year's flowering right after it blooms. The bulb below ground is "re-charged" by the foliage that remains after flowering; if you lop off green foliage, the bulb may not flower next season.

IF YOU MUST...
TRANSPLANT SPENT BULBS, TAKE GENEROUS BALL OF EARTH WITH EACH

HEEL THEM IN ELSEWHERE IN THE GARDEN

BETTER YET...
FOLD FOLIAGE, TIE WITH RUBBER BAND

OR STAPLE IT DOWN WITH WIRE HAIRPINS

PLANT SHALLOW-ROOTED ANNUAL PHLOX OVER

If you must transplant bulbs while foliage is still green, be sure to take a sizable piece of earth with each bulb, and move them to their new location to be watered only until leaves have died down. A better practice is to heel them in, in some inconspicuous corner; keep them watered while they cure, then dig and store them until the proper planting time.

Most gardeners, rather than digging bulbs, fold the foliage and bind it with a rubber band, or pin it flat to the ground with a hairpin-shaped piece of wire. A shallow-rooted annual such as dwarf phlox, planted between the bulbs, will grow quickly to a low blanket of color over the browning foliage.

PERENNIALS

Timing and *immediate transplanting* are the two most important factors to be considered when transplanting perennials.

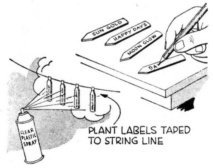

IF YOU CAN'T DIVIDE AND REPLANT THE SAME DAY, COVER CLUMPS WITH WET BURLAP...

OR HEEL IN CLUMPS IN TRENCHES & COVER ROOTS WITH DAMP SOIL

GATHER UP CORNERS AND TIE, THEN SET BAG IN SHADE UNTIL YOU CAN PLANT— PLASTIC BAGS KEEP ROOTS MOIST

Spring and early summer flowering perennials may be dug and transplanted in the early fall. Late blooming kinds, such as chrysanthemums, may be transplanted in early winter, if you live in a mild climate; in cold-winter areas, wait until spring.

Don't let roots dry out while you are transplanting. If you can't replant the same day, cover the clumps with wet burlap or wrap them in polyethylene.

LABELLING PLANTS

For the little time and trouble they involve, plant labels are well worthwhile. Many a gardener has had the frustrating experience of wondering what to do for a certain plant, yet being stopped from the very start because of not knowing its name and—therefore—its cultural needs.

Even if you have very few shrubs and trees, and are sure you know what they are, you will find plant labels handy for identifying annuals or vegetables and their varieties. You'll get to know your favorites by name, and there'll be no head-scratching in case you wish to plant some more of them next season.

Plant labels are available in nurseries and garden stores; or you can make your own. (Sticks on ice cream bars and frozen juice bars make good labels, as do tongue-depressers.) Labels for container plants and beds of annuals may simply be inserted in the dirt next to the plants, with the name showing. For larger, more permanent plantings, it is better to attach the label loosely.

PLANT LABELS TAPED TO STRING LINE

If you mark labels *with pencil, coat them with a clear, non-toxic plastic so names won't fade in sun or wash off.*

Plant names *burned into wood labels with an electric burning device will remain legible; no coating necessary.*

PHLOX - Divide Nov. Move to SW corner in front of clematis
Bloomed June 20 - Good cerise - Cut back July
Repeat bloom Sept. 15
SPRAY - for mildew
Moved Nov - 5

Large labels *are handy for keeping garden records. After bloom, you can transfer information to a notebook.*

GIRDLING AROUND LABEL WIRE

USE COFFEE STIRRER OR...

TIE LABEL WIRE ON WITH SOFT TWINE

Stout wire *can choke a plant as it grows. Use light wire or twine, attach it to a branch rather than the trunk.*

FALL PLANTING ... IDEAL FOR MILD CLIMATES

The fall-to-spring sequence illustrated below demonstrates a fact we think isn't well enough known to many gardeners. To wit: Spring may be the season for all kinds of planting in climates where ground freezes in the winter, but in mild regions the smart time to plant most things is in the fall—in order to follow the heat, get ahead of the cold, take advantage of winter rains, and anticipate the spring growth surge.

In low desert areas, gardeners and nurserymen know and live by this timing. Summers are so hot in that climate that when fall comes, it's "everybody out for planting." The fact is that gardeners in any mild-winter region would do well to follow this same procedure.

California is one of several states where a gardener can benefit from the advantages of fall planting. To quote from *Sunset Magazine*, the acknowledged authority on gardening in the West:

"We think that all California gardeners, especially newcomers, should realize again the opportunity that fall offers, and take advantage of it. People accustomed to the autumns of colder climates seem to feel that we don't really have an autumn here. We do—but it is subtle, and it takes a while to become sensitive to its subtleties. As days shorten, nights become noticeably cooler, and even the summer-like daytime air has a different feeling about it. But the soil retains warmth into the late fall."

As you can see in the drawings below, it's the combination of several factors—autumn's warm soil, falling night tem-

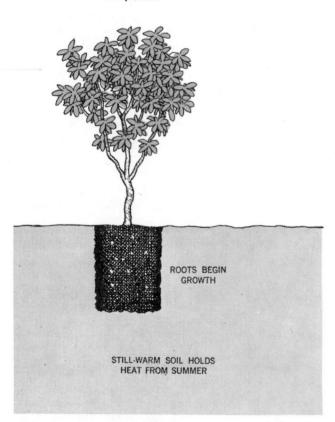

FALL
COOLING AIR

Fall-planted

ROOTS BEGIN
GROWTH

STILL-WARM SOIL HOLDS
HEAT FROM SUMMER

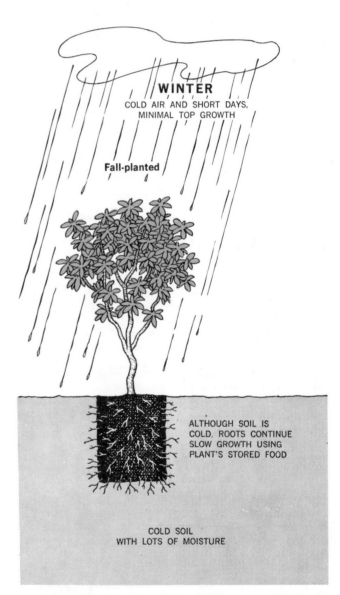

WINTER
COLD AIR AND SHORT DAYS,
MINIMAL TOP GROWTH

Fall-planted

ALTHOUGH SOIL IS
COLD, ROOTS CONTINUE
SLOW GROWTH USING
PLANT'S STORED FOOD

COLD SOIL
WITH LOTS OF MOISTURE

By planting *any of a long list of plants in fall (a shrub, in this example) you can take advantage of the seasons. Soil is still warm, encouraging root growth. Because of cooler air, plants will lose less moisture through the leaves.*

In winter, *short days and low temperatures bring most top growth to a stop; roots are less sensitive to temperatures (as long as above freezing), and continue growth that started when soil was warm. By spring, roots are well established.*

peratures, the rains that will come in winter, and the lack of soil freezing—that makes our fall season so good for planting.

It's easy to tell which are the plants that should *not* be planted in fall. They are the tender plants that might be killed or damaged by winter frosts. Some classic examples are citrus, Chinese hibiscus, tropical ferns, bougainvilleas, lantana; add to the list any other shrub or tree of borderline hardiness. If your area gets no frosts, there of course are no limitations at all.

Let's look at the many kinds of plants that do benefit from fall planting:

Annuals. Early autumn (preferably the last 2 weeks in September) are preferable for planting calendulas, Iceland poppies, snapdragons, stock, and African daisies, if you want to try for midwinter flowering.

Perennials. Fall is the best time to plant all spring and early summer flowering perennials.

Shrubs. Just a few of the many are: azalea, camellia, ceanothus, all conifers, daphne, privet, rhododendron, roses from containers, and lilac.

Trees. As with shrubs, nearly all trees may be planted in fall. There's a special bonus with fruit trees and other deciduous trees that were put into cans at the end of the previous bare-root season. All spring and summer, they formed hair roots in the cans; these hair roots are ready to grow with fall planting.

Ground covers. Chamomile, Mondo grass, dwarf rosemary, strawberry, and star jasmine are some of the many ground covers that can be planted in fall.

Hardy grass lawns. October is an ideal time to plant mixes and straights containing any of the bluegrasses, fescues, and bents. However, dichondra and tropical grasses such as zoysia and Bermuda should not be sown until spring.

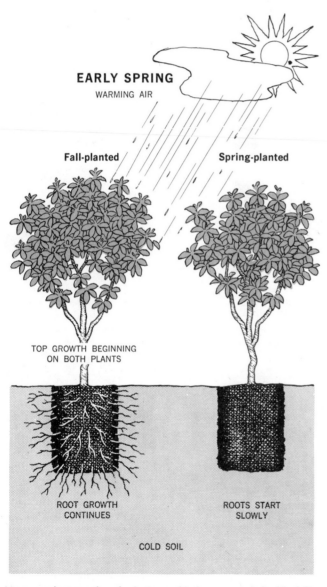

EARLY SPRING
WARMING AIR

Fall-planted   Spring-planted

TOP GROWTH BEGINNING ON BOTH PLANTS

ROOT GROWTH CONTINUES   ROOTS START SLOWLY

COLD SOIL

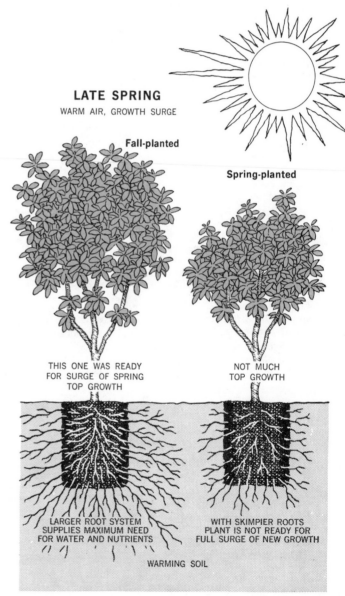

LATE SPRING
WARM AIR, GROWTH SURGE

Fall-planted   Spring-planted

THIS ONE WAS READY FOR SURGE OF SPRING TOP GROWTH   NOT MUCH TOP GROWTH

LARGER ROOT SYSTEM SUPPLIES MAXIMUM NEED FOR WATER AND NUTRIENTS   WITH SKIMPIER ROOTS PLANT IS NOT READY FOR FULL SURGE OF NEW GROWTH

WARMING SOIL

Now we plant another shrub *(same kind, same age) beside fall-planted shrub. At first, only roots new one has are those in root ball. Cold soil doesn't encourage fast start. Fall planted shrub has roots out in surrounding soil.*

Here is the payoff from fall planting. *Difference is more than just a 4-month calendar advantage. With more roots, fall-planted shrub can now supply leaves with adequate moisture when hot days bring about rapid water loss.*

PLANTING A LAWN

Each of the pre-planting steps described here is generally recognized as being essential to building a lawn that will perform for many years to come. You can short-cut the installation procedure with abandon if you want a lawn of temporary nature, if the lawn you are building can be second or third-rate in quality, or if you live in an especially favored climate.

Making a good lawn the right way is not easy. But each step

1. *If your soil is acid enough to limit growth (pH below 5.5), neutralize it by applying lime (agricultural lime) at the rate of 50 to 75 pounds per 1,000 square feet per application. Apply on dry soil with a spreader. Prevent chemical from contacting roots of acid-loving shrubs.*

If you have an alkali soil, you can use one of several products to reduce the alkalinity and at the same time improve soil structure. Actually, you should strive to lower pH only if it is above 8.3 or 8.4.

Gypsum is the most widely used for this purpose. It has the advantage of practically limitless safe application. About 35 to 50 pounds per 1,000 square feet will usually suffice.

2. *For soils too sandy or too clayey, add organic matter to the soil—products such as sawdust, ground bark, peat moss. For truly effective results, you should apply enough on soil so you can work in more than 30% by volume (see page 4).*

3. *Rotary till the soil conditioner into the soil as deep as possible (some tillers will go as deep as 6 to 9 inches, and that is desirable). Make several trips over the area with the tiller in order to make a completely uniform blending.*

4. *Pick out debris after cultivating and again after lawn bed is raked, smoothed, and leveled. Get rid of every stone, stick, and foreign object on surface. Take out clumps of old grass and weeds, too. (Old lawns should be scraped off before tilling.)*

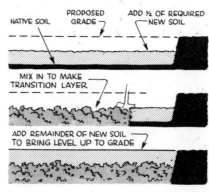

5. *When it is necessary to bring in topsoil, make a blended layer between it and the native soil. First, mix half the total topsoil with native soil. Then add the rest of the topsoil over the blended layer to bring the level up to grade.*

6. *A cultivated lawn bed will have a rolling and uneven surface. Roll it first with a light roller to define low and high spots. Once you've found them, drag or push soil from high spots into low areas with one of these implements.*

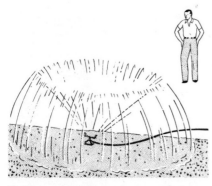

7. *If you want to make sure that your lawn bed will be as weed-free and disease-free as possible, treat now with Vapam or Mylone, or at step 3 and now with calcium cyanamid. Or, you can water now to bring up the weeds.*

8. *A two week watering period after step #7 will, in addition to bringing up weeds, settle some low spots. At this point then, you can pull the germinated weeds and fill the sunken spots in (or knock off high spots) to make entire surface level.*

9. *Before fertilizing and seeding, roll the lawn bed one more time to give it a smooth surface. The roller at this stage should be light (either empty or filled with just a few inches of water), especially if soil is moist.*

in the process leads to avoiding a familiar shortcoming of bad, old lawns. For instance, careful grading makes good drainage so your lawn won't puddle and develop spots that are waterlogged and soft, or hard and dry. Digging in organic matter and other soil amendments makes a rich, somewhat self-sufficient root area. Blending topsoil with native soil to make a transitional layer between topsoil and native soil avoids trapping roots in a shallow topsoil basin in which they would be dependent on frequent feeding and very frequent watering.

For information on the various kinds of lawn grasses, see page 110.

10. *Get enough complete commercial fertilizer to cover the area according to label directions for new lawns. A good spreader will do the job perfectly. Be sure that each trail of fertilizer exactly meets trail beside it.*

11. *Use a mechanical seeder, or sow by hand. If you do it by hand, broadcast one quarter portion of the seed evenly down each half of the lawn. Divide lawn in half in opposite direction and sow remaining quarter portions on these two halves.*

12. *After the seed is broadcast, rake it in lightly to insure a thorough contact of seed with seedbed soil. Very lightly brush up the seeded surface with a wire rake—use light circular motions. Swirl any patches of seeds out evenly.*

13. *After seeding and cross-raking, put on a seed-protecting mulch — a 1/8 to 3/16-inch layer of peat moss or screened sawdust. Scatter the mulch on as evenly as possible. Don't toss it upward so that it falls in piles.*

14. *Roll the mulch over the seeds with a light empty roller. This step can be skipped, but it is a nice extra. Wear tennis shoes, if possible, so you don't make heel impressions. Seedbed won't be walked on again for several weeks.*

15. *Keep the mulch dark with moisture until all the grasses are up. This may take up to three weeks if your seed mix includes slow-germinating varieties. Use a hand sprinkler on a lawn seedbed if it's convenient. Set systems cause washouts.*

16. *After the first week, the little seedlings will have gained enough stature to take a bending. It is possible, and often advisable at that time, to pull the weeds that come up with seeds. Lay a wide plank over young grass; stand on it to weed.*

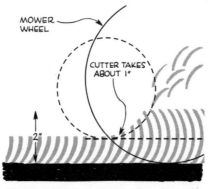

17. *Mow the lawn for the first time when the grass is about two inches high. Or, mow when the grass blades get tall enough to take on a noticeable curvature. Bent grasses should never be allowed to grow higher than 1 inch.*

18. *Place string barrier around the new lawn as soon as you finish sowing it. Keep it around the lawn until 8 weeks after the first mowing. The barrier should be adequate to keep people and dogs off the seedbed and the new grass.*

PLANTING A HEDGE

The possibilities of the hedge go far beyond the old idea that it is nothing more than a substitute for a fence to separate your garden from your neighbor's or to provide a barrier between your front yard and the street. Solid lines of one kind of shrub can be used as base plantings next to the house; patio enclosures; free-standing sound, dust, and wind barriers; traffic stoppers; dividers between sections of the garden; and in many other ways.

Be sure to choose the right plant. Never put in larger plants for quick effect and expect to keep them low by cutting them back—eventually, they'll get away from you.

The following hardy shrubs make excellent hedges; however, be sure to check with a local nurseryman for names of other hedge plants which do well in your region.

Boxwood (Buxus). Evergreen. Some varieties of *Buxus microphylla* are outstanding. Moderate growers (to 3 feet); good formal hedges.

Yew (Taxus). Evergreen. Many good varieties, all heights. Can clip to any shape.

Privet. Evergreen, deciduous species. Many sizes. All have beautiful creamy-white flowers. *Ligustrum vulgare* (common privet or English privet) is an exceptionally good deciduous type; a dwarf form is available.

Thuja. Evergreen. These conifers are neat, compact growers. Many species and sizes, some less than a foot high.

Planting distance apart varies by species. As a rule-of-thumb: If your hedge is to be 6 feet high, space plants 3 feet apart; if you plant a low grower and want a 1-foot hedge, space 1 foot apart. Spacing for heights in between should be from 1 to 3 feet.

Informal hedges need only an annual trimming, but you'll have to clip frequently if you want to shape the plants formally. Keep hedges wider at the bottom than at the top to permit sunlight to reach the bases of the plants and to encourage vigorous growth.

Remember to consider your neighbor in the event you plant a hedge along your property line. Also, be sure to check your local ordinances as to height restrictions.

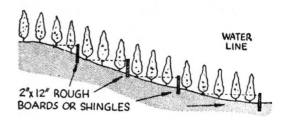

Water will run down hedge trench on slopes unless you hold it back in some way. You can use soil, shingles, boards.

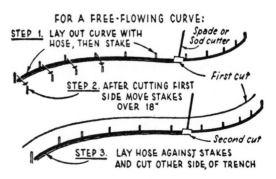

To lay out planting trench for free-flowing curved hedge, use pliable hose; mark the trench sides as shown.

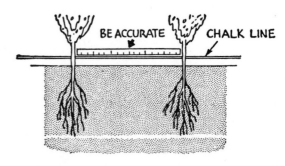

Planting distances vary according to plant size, type of hedge. Plants are usually set closer for formal hedges.

PLANTING CAMELLIAS . . . WATER LILIES

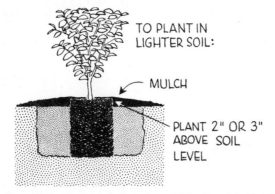

Camellias. *Make planting hole twice width of root ball; plant slightly high. If your native soil is heavy clay or adobe, plant with half of root ball above soil level and heap mulch around it. Always use light soil mix for camellias, rhododendrons, azaleas.*

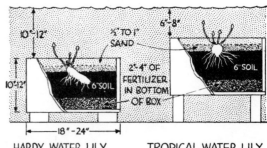

Water lilies. *Plant these, other aquatic plants in containers that can be submerged, taken out for replanting every 3 years. Plant hardy types in spring, tropicals when weather and water warm up. Tropicals should be closer to water surface.*

CHAPTER 4

Watering Your Garden

DARROW M. WATT

WHAT SIZE GARDEN HOSE?

Garden hoses, as you can see by these photographs, come in different sizes—and in this instance, we mean *diameter*, an important consideration that many gardeners fail to comprehend until after they've made their purchase. Regardless of what your water pressure happens to be, the output you get from it through a hose is in direct ratio to the hose's inside diameter.

The smallest diameter commonly sold—7/16 inch—is too small to be recommended for general gardening use, so we don't consider it here. Standard sizes are 1/2, 5/8, and 3/4-inch diameter. A hose of 1-inch diameter is manufactured, but it's difficult to use and is seldom sold to home gardeners.

When you buy a hose, avoid the super-bargains—they seldom last very long, and can cause you much trouble and lost time. The best indication of a good hose is a guarantee. Don't buy one that isn't guaranteed or warranted. It's that simple.

½-inch hose	⅝-inch hose	¾-inch hose

In 15 seconds, *a 50-foot length of ½-inch hose filled this 5-gallon jar approximately 1/3 full. If you have big, thirsty trees and shrubs to water, buy a larger size.*

A 50-foot *length of ⅝-inch hose delivered twice the amount of water as the size at left, in same period of time. This size is practical for almost any home garden.*

Big ¾-inch hose, 50 feet, filled jar in 15 seconds. *With pressure of 50 pounds per square inch, it put an inch of water on 1,500-sq. ft. lawn in 39 minutes.*

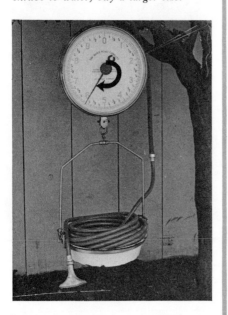

DARROW M. WATT

Advantages *of ½-inch size are light weight (6 pounds), easy storage. Fine for watering container plants; well suited for women's and children's use.*

Middle-sized *⅝-inch hose weighs only 1½ pounds more than size at left, sells best in regions with fairly large lots or low water pressure.*

"*Big daddy*" *of garden hoses, ¾-inch size is heavy (11 pounds) and hard to store. It's long wearing, and is a necessity with some kinds of sprinklers.*

LAWN WATERING

Choosing a sprinkler can be a dilemma to the home gardener, what with the ever-increasing variety of kinds to select from.

Generally, however, different sprinklers can be grouped according to the kind of watering pattern they make. A study of the five patterns shown here should help you to decide which sprinkler might be the best one for you.

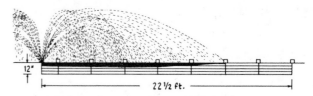
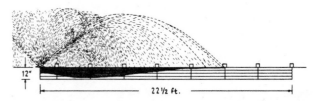

3. Useful but erratic; most of water falls from 4 to 8 feet out. Some examples: plastic tube soakers; types with slowly revolving arms; those which squirt water from sieve holes.

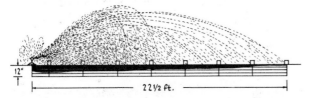

1. Effective, if you move sprinkler to obtain overlap. Oscillating type makes this pattern, as does rotating impulse or "machine gun" type, which shoots rapid-fire jets.

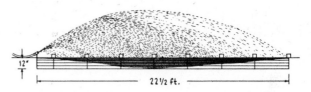

4. Cone spray soaks only a small area; for best results, turn water to half-pressure, move sprinkler often. One sprinkler of this type has two big holes like owl's eyes.

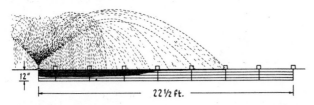

2. Most water drops on inside; you must make successive overlaps. Several sprinklers work this way, including "fixed head" types and those with whirling baffle on top.

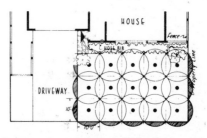

5. Fan spray throws most water 7 to 14 feet from sprinkler head. Example: nailhead spike type, which sprays water through a slit in its head. Useful for odd corners.

A good sprinkler system requires careful planning . . .

An underground sprinkler system is well worth the initial trouble and expense if you qualify on any of these counts:

1. Your lawn is large or odd-shaped.

2. Other chores do not allow you the time to move sprinklers around.

3. You simply do not like to water.

Galvanized iron pipe was, for many years, by far the most popular material for sprinkler systems. It is still popular and widely used, despite its expense and difficulty of installation.

During recent years, plastic and other non-metallic systems have gained great favor with many home gardeners. They are long lasting, much less expensive than metal types, and quite simple for the average homeowner to install himself. They can be tested above ground before installation. It is simpler to put a system of this type into an already-existing lawn (only a narrow trench need be dug).

Regardless of which type you install, the spray pattern is all-important. To the right are four good examples.

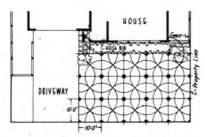

Complete coverage *using eight full circle heads, eleven ½ circle heads, one ¾ circle head, three ¼ circle heads.*

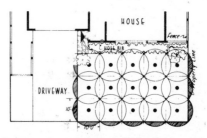

Layout *using 14 full circle heads, one ¾ circle head. Gives complete coverage, but wastes some water around edges.*

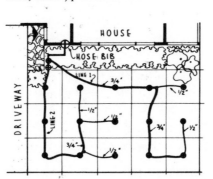

With flexible pipe, *you can make a layout like this. You can use any pattern, running around any obstacles.*

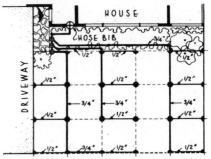

Branch pattern *works with any pipe. This design is for 3 lines because of pressure drop due to numerous fittings.*

WATERING TECHNIQUES

Dry-season watering is the biggest task home gardeners face; it's the obligation you must accept once you start to garden. Some find it a time-consuming chore they'd just as soon avoid, so they install automatic sprinklers that do the work for them. Others enjoy it. They like to get outside to observe their plants at close hand, and don't mind moving the sprinkler every so often across the lawn or from one garden bed to another.

Of course it takes more than just water to keep a garden looking its best. It needs fertilizer and cultivation, and freedom from weeds and pests. But water is the one thing we tend to misuse most. We use too much, too little, or waste it in half a dozen ways.

Fresh water is a relatively scarce commodity, and some communities have, in the past, experienced some restrictions on its use. But our object here is not to forecast whether, when, and where water consumption will be regulated. It is to point up ways to get the greatest good from any water you give your garden.

THE BEST TIME TO WATER

Plants transpire (lose water through their leaves) most when temperatures are high, with the greatest loss between noon and 3 P.M. Although roots do absorb water both day and night, on a hot day transpiration may exceed absorption. If the loss is too great, leaves wilt. However, if there's enough moisture in the soil, the moisture content in the leaves will go back to normal at night. Watering in the evening is therefore the best way to get water into the soil without undue loss through evaporation. There's also little or no moisture loss through surface evaporation during the night.

Watering in the evening also gives you the benefit of high water pressure. In most communities, the greatest draw on water is between 8 A.M. and 6 to 8 P.M.,

WATER PRESSURE HIGHEST 6:00 TO 8:00AM OR AFTER 6:00PM BIGGEST DEMAND FROM 8:00 AM TO 6:00 PM

so sprinklers work at peak efficiency later in the evening or early morning. (For plants susceptible to mildew, morning watering is best so leaves dry out before night.)

WIND WASTES WATER

Summer winds often disrupt the pattern of a sprinkler system, and sections of lawn or garden beds on the windward

WATER WHEN AIR IS STILL TO PREVENT WASTE

side may not get their fair share. So watering in the morning or evening is most efficient on another count—little or no wind.

DO YOU WATER TOO MUCH?

Next weekend, look around your neighborhood at the condition of lawns, shrubs, and trees. In most cases all the gardens will look in about the same state of greenness. But if you charted the amount of time your neighbors spend on watering, it would vary a good deal from house to house. The man on the corner may run his sprinklers all weekend, regardless of the weather. The place next door looks as good, but gets only half as much water.

Soils can take only so much water. Clay or adobe holds moisture like a sponge and can absorb about three times as much water as sand. Therefore, you'll have to water sandy soil more often than clay. The only sure way to know whether to water is to test the soil. Dig down about 18 inches and see if the subsoil is moist.

A simpler method is to buy a soil sampler. There are two kinds. One is a cylinder with one side open; you push it into the soil, pull it up with a core of soil enclosed, and knock the core out to study it. The other is an auger that takes soil up and out of the ground in the same way that a wood drill brings up wood chips. Soil tubes and augers will take cores down to three feet deep. You can even eliminate this bother by installing a moisture indicator. Tied in with a sprinkler system, the moisture indicator turns the water on and off when the soil reaches a certain degree

TEST SOIL TO SEE IF IT NEEDS WATER

of dryness. You avoid overwatering and underwatering.

TREE ROOTS COMPETE FOR WATER

Spade around shrubs growing close to trees and chances are you'll find a net-

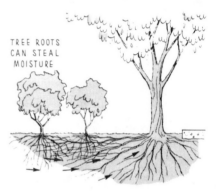

TREE ROOTS CAN STEAL MOISTURE

work of roots that the tree has sent out to tap the moisture supply in frequently watered beds. This is particularly true if the tree is along the street or in some other location that doesn't get regular watering. Cultivating the soil between the shrubs and the tree two or three times during the season will sever these roots and reduce the competition. Giving the tree its own water rations will help, too.

THE GOOD OF A WATER BASIN

The more surface area you water, the greater the evaporation. For example,

WATER BASINS DIRECT WATER TO ROOT ZONE

if you have an orchard of small trees spaced 20 feet apart, and individual trees spread no wider than 3 feet, it doesn't make sense to water the entire orchard with a sprinkler. The root zone of the trees doesn't extend much beyond the drip line. While the trees are still small, it's wise to prepare a basin around each tree and fill it with a hose. This confines the water to a small area and reduces evaporation.

VALUABLE MULCHES

A mulch can reduce the amount of water lost through surface evaporation by about half. Tests show that a mulch 2 to 3 inches deep actually insulates the soil; it slows the increase in soil temperature, reduces evaporation, and therefore, promotes root growth in the top 6 or so inches—the richest and best aerated soil in the whole garden. Without a protective mulch cover (or without a substantial amount of humus added), the top soil layer gets so hot that roots burn out. It the plant isn't killed, the shock may arrest growth. If temperatures are consistently high, roots won't even grow into this zone. (Most roots grow best when soil temperatures are between 60° and 70°.)

2" TO 3" MULCH KEEPS SOIL COOL, MOIST

Mulches of some kind are sold almost everywhere. Peat moss is probably the most widely distributed, but commercially packaged ground or shredded bark and sawdust are also widely available. In some areas you can buy mulching materials that are by-products of local industries: hops, rice hulls, yucca fiber, wood chips, sawdust and shredded bark, spent mushroom compost, manures. Some of these you can purchase by the truckful at substantial savings; much of the cost is transportation.

One caution if you use *fresh* ground bark or sawdust: As it breaks down, it draws nitrogen from the soil—nitrogen needed by the plants. To offset this, add about 2 to 3 pounds of a high nitrogen fertilizer to each 1-inch layer of sawdust spread over 100 square feet of ground. Some packagers of these materials now fortify the material with nitrogen, thereby saving you the trouble.

LESS WATER RUN-OFF IN POROUS SOIL

Water will run off compacted soil long before the soil is saturated. Compacted lawn areas tend to cause the most trouble. If you run the sprinklers only until you see run-off or puddling, chances are good that the root zone is still dry. Here the soil tube or auger comes in handy. By taking out a sample core of soil, you can see how much thatch has built up and to what degree the soil is compacted. Best treatment is to aerate the soil; open it up by coring to let in water, air, and fertilizer. (If water can't penetrate the soil, fertilizer and air can't either.)

LESS RUN-OFF IN POROUS SOIL ADD HUMUS MATERIAL

On open beds you can see compacted soil. Spade it up and add a soil conditioner (see pages 4 and 5); spread a 3-inch layer over the ground and work it into the top 6 to 8 inches of soil. This will increase the moisture holding capacity of sandy soils and make clay soils more porous. A porous soil will also absorb winter rains more readily, replenishing the soil moisture reserves.

WEEDS STEAL WATER

Moisture is lost from the ground in two ways: by surface evaporation from the top six or so inches of soil and by the process of transpiration by which plants absorb water through their roots and give it off to the air through their leaves. Weeds rob soil moisture; some do much more than others. A mustard weed plant uses up four times as much water as a single oat plant. (Weeds also rob valuable nutrients. That same mus-

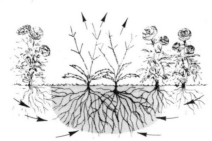

WEEDS DRAW OFF VALUABLE SOIL MOISTURE

tard plant may use up twice the nitrogen and phosphorus and four times as much potassium as the oat.) A thick mulch will also deter weed growth.

SHELTERS FOR SHADE PLANTS

Adjusting to the various water needs of plants scattered about the garden is

GROW SHADE- AND MOISTURE-LOVING PLANTS IN PROTECTED AREAS

a nuisance. But if you plant all your moisture-loving plants in a bed sheltered from the sun and drying winds, you will save both water and time. Also, in hot dry areas, it's about the only way you can successfully grow such plants as fuchsias, tuberous begonias, and hydrangeas.

KEEPING CONTAINER PLANTS WATERED

If you have many plants in containers, you'll find that pot-bound ones dry out fastest. Roots fill every inch of space and there is no soil left to hold moisture. Either move these plants into larger containers or shave the root ball, add fresh soil, and put the plant back in the same pot. You'll soon see a difference.

POT-BOUND PLANTS HAVE NO RESERVE SOIL MOISTURE

To keep container plants from drying out while you are on vacation, water them well and sink the pots into moist soil or peat in a shady spot. To cut down the rate of evaporation through the sides of clay pots, wrap the pots with metal foil (if you don't have too many) or paint the outside with a clear masonry sealer. Or put a small pot inside a larger one and fill the space between with wet peat.

WATERING PLANTS IN CONTAINERS

The subject of watering plants growing in containers may seem almost too basic to mention. However, if you've ever nursed a dozen or so through a hot summer, you know it's not so simple.

We can't say how often to water; that depends on such variables as soil mix, type of container, its location in the garden, and climate. In most situations the soil in a container dries out much faster than in a garden bed, and you may have to water every day during hot spells.

Here are some methods for doing the job efficiently:

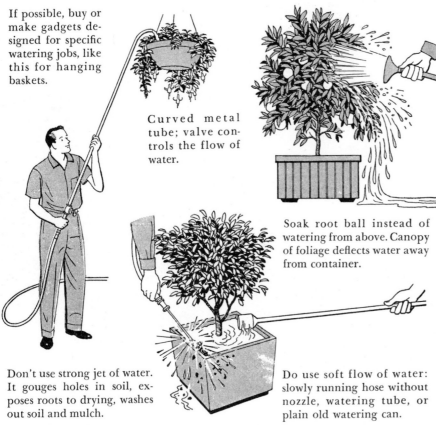

If possible, buy or make gadgets designed for specific watering jobs, like this for hanging baskets.

Curved metal tube; valve controls the flow of water.

Don't use strong jet of water. It gouges holes in soil, exposes roots to drying, washes out soil and mulch.

Soak root ball instead of watering from above. Canopy of foliage deflects water away from container.

Do use soft flow of water: slowly running hose without nozzle, watering tube, or plain old watering can.

Sometimes you can water a plant every day and it still wilts. When a root ball gets too dry, it tends to shrink away from sides of the container, leaving a narrow crack. You add water, but instead of soaking into root ball, it runs down cracks and out bottom drain holes.

To prevent this, scratch soil surface around edge with hand cultivator, screwdriver, or sharp stick, filling crack with loosened soil; or add fresh soil, then soak with water until root ball is saturated. If container is small, submerge in bucket of water until air bubbles stop.

DRAIN HOLE

Placing cork in drain hole makes thorough watering possible without moving basket.

BASIN
WATER
FLOWER POT

Basket submerged in water. Inverted pot prevents harm to hanging branches.

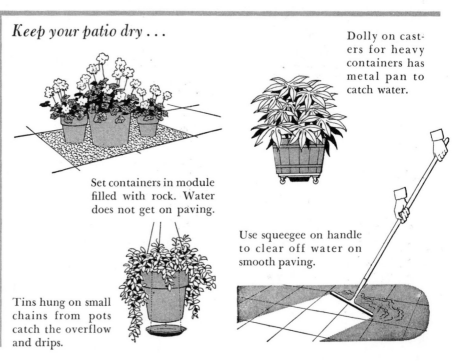

Keep your patio dry . . .

Set containers in module filled with rock. Water does not get on paving.

Tins hung on small chains from pots catch the overflow and drips.

Dolly on casters for heavy containers has metal pan to catch water.

Use squeegee on handle to clear off water on smooth paving.

CHAPTER 5

Fertilizing Techniques

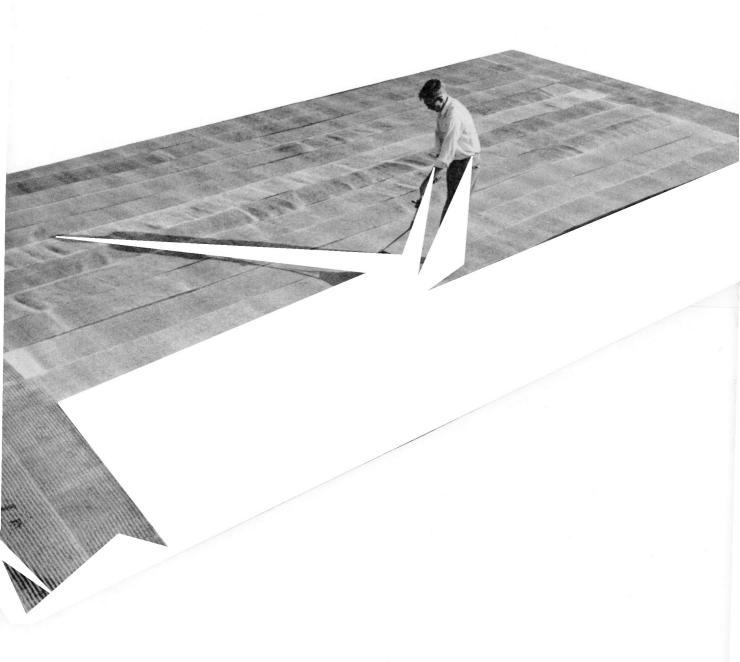

FERTILIZERS...
AND HOW TO USE THEM

Fertilizer is not just a single-purpose substance like the gasoline you put in your car or the sugar you mix into a cake batter. Fertilizer is a combination of chemicals, and each part of the combination goes to work in a different way. Some of the chemicals in the fertilizer you apply may do a great deal of good; others may do little or nothing for *your* plants in *your* soil.

If you are an inquiring gardener, curious about what goes on in the soil and inside the plant after you apply fertilizer, you will find some facts on these pages that will make plant nutrition more understandable. They may even start you on your way toward becoming a real dietitian for your plants.

WHAT IS A "COMPLETE" FERTILIZER?

Any fertilizer that contains all three of the essential food elements—nitrogen, phosphorus, and potassium—is known as a complete fertilizer.

You probably have one or more sacks, boxes, or bottles of complete fertilizer in your garage or on your gardening shelf right now. And good that you do. Almost all plants in almost all soils need it repeatedly in order to grow and bloom to perfection.

Fertilizer men talk of the elements nitrogen, phosphorus, and potassium by their chemical symbols N, P, and K respectively. Gardeners and farmers use another shortened term—three numbers in a row representing the percentages of N, P, and K.

Some fertilizer manufacturers put their analysis percentages in big numbers on the label, right under the product name. Or perhaps the label reads something like this:

Without looking at the fine print under *Guaranteed Analysis*, you can tell that "Feed-em" contains 10 per cent total nitrogen, 8 per cent phosphoric acid, and 6 per cent water-soluble potash.

Actually, there are many different analyses; however, even when the analysis is the same on two different products, the formula or "recipe" by which one manufacturer arrived at his analysis can differ from the others.

Total food units. Fertilizer prices are directly related to total units of plant food. Generally, the higher the total, the higher the cost. If the total is high, the label directs you to put proportionately less fertilizer on each 100 square feet of soil. It's only reasonable that a 20-20-10 percentage would call for half as much fertilizer per square foot as a 10-10-10.

The reason the total units never reach anywhere near 100 per cent is that each of the NPK elements uses other compounds as carriers. You will always buy a certain amount of other material with a fertilizer. You'll remember from your chemistry classes that pure nitrogen is a gas, pure phosphorus is a glowing substance, pure potassium is a strange-acting metal. You could hardly put the three in a package in their pure form

Special purpose plant foods. We've noticed another trend—toward packaging complete fertilizer as "Camellia Food," "Rhododendron Food," or "Rose Food." The camellia and rhododendron foods join an old established group—the acid plant foods. Some of the compounds used in these fertilizers are chosen because they have an acid reaction.

Of most products packaged for other plants, we can't say what NPK ratios are ideally suited because different products marked for the same plants vary too much in their NPK ratios.

True organic fertilizers. Cottonseed meal, blood meal, bonemeal, and similar organic fertilizers have their NPK ratios stated on the labels. Most are high in just one of the three elements, low or zero in the other two. But, tradition says, they are useful for specific purposes.

Manure is a complete fertilizer, but weak when judged on NPK standards. Manures vary in their nutrient content according to the animal and what the animal had been eating. But an NPK ratio of approximately 1-1-1 is typical. Manure never registers as high as the mildest of complete chemical fertilizers.

However, it's not the fertilizer function alone for which you apply manure to a garden bed. The value of its 40 to 60 per cent organic matter is tremendous. Organic matter plays a part in the holding and release of soil and fertilizer nutrients. From a strictly physical standpoint, manure and other bulky organic fertilizers help, too, making soil stay open and workable.

Among other reactions, manure increases the availability of phosphorus. Mixing superphosphate with manure before it is put on the soil makes the superphosphate more efficient.

TIMING A FEEDING

When you realize what can happen in 12 months to the fertilizer you apply this month, you see why one feeding is seldom adequate. The nitrogen that isn't used by plants can be leached out by watering and used up by soil organisms. The phosphorus may have been just enough to satisfy the hungry minerals that "fix" it, leaving the roots to get what soil phosphorus they can. The soluble potassium may be used up rapidly, creating a hard pull on what exchangeable potassium exists in the soil.

If your fertilizer carries no instructions on it for repeating application, use these suggestions as a general guide:

Feed roses with label-recommended amounts every six weeks, from early spring to late summer.

Feed rhododendrons, azaleas, and camellias immediately after bloom, and again in 6 weeks.

4" FROM ROOTS

Dry fertilizer. *If area is dug but not planted, work fertilizer into future root zone. If young plants are already in, apply in bands on both sides, 4 inches from roots.*

Liquid fertilizer. *Young annuals and vegetables like a high-nitrogen feeding. Apply in basins (as shown here) or rows, several inches from base of plants; then water.*

Feed fuchsias, begonias, and other lush, verdant, summer-time flower producers every 4 to 6 weeks with label-recommended doses, or once every 2 or 3 weeks with half doses.

Fruit trees can take nutrients almost any time, but the time of greatest need is about 2 or 3 weeks before blossoming.

Big, old garden trees can be fed by the holes-around-the-dripline method once a year if you think they need it (see page 55). Young trees and fast-growing, surface-rooting trees like willows can be fed on the surface, as the labels suggest for shrubs.

Most vegetable crops—corn, tomatoes, and leaf crops in particular—need a starter fertilizer at planting time. In addition, it's helpful to give them additional nitrogen (or a complete fertilizer if it's handier) after they are well started.

For anything else, feed when you see growth starting, again in summer, and—in mild climates or with definitely hardy plants—feed once more in the fall.

Below, we discuss the characteristics of the three essential plant food elements, as well as some of the lesser ones.

NITROGEN

In the natural course of events (with no fertilizer added), nitrogen that comes into the soil as dead plant or animal material must undergo several chemical changes before it becomes available to plants' roots.

Microörganisms must digest organic nitrogen and convert it to ammonia, a form of nitrogen. Another set of microörganisms must change ammonia to the nitrite form of nitrogen. And, finally, nitrite nitrogen must be changed by microörganisms to nitrate nitrogen. Plants can only use nitrogen when it is in the ammonia or nitrate form. The organisms that do the converting use a certain amount of the nitrogen to build the tissue of their own bodies.

Most of the nitrogen in complete fertilizers is in the organic form, either natural or synthetic. A good number of complete fertilizers contain nitrogen in the ammonia form. A few contain nitrogen in the nitrate form.

If a fertilizer's label says that all or most of the nitrogen contained is in the nitrate (or nitric) form, you know it will be fast acting. On the other hand, if it's mostly ammonic or

organic, the response will be not quite as fast, but it should be more sustained once it starts. The ammonic nitrogen should cause a faster response than organic nitrogen.

The fast response is much more noticeable and significant in lawns than in plants and trees, though it applies to all. It's also easy to burn a lawn by putting on too much nitrogen, since grass is made up of thousands of tiny plants growing together. Shrub roots grow deep and wide and have more soil around them to act as a buffer.

Not a mineral. Nitrogen is not present in the minute particles of mineral soil from which plants get their phosphorus, potassium, and the 10 other mineral elements. All nitrogen must come from the air (some of which gets into soil via rainfall), from organic matter, or from fertilizers. As a fertilizer, nitrogen (the nitrate form) leaches through the root area fast.

Carbon-nitrogen ratio. If organic matter that you add to the soil is high in carbon compared to nitrogen, soil organisms working to digest the high carbon material may compete with the crops for nitrogen. That is why wise gardeners add ammonium sulfate or a complete fertilizer to sawdust, shavings, or straw used as a mulch or a soil conditioner. (Mix in $1\frac{1}{8}$ pounds ammonium sulfate per 100 square feet for every inch of mulch.) The supplementary nitrogen keeps the carbon-nitrogen ratio in balance.

What nitrogen does. The nitrogen in soil regulates a plant's ability to make proteins that are vital to formation of new protoplasm in the cells. Even the important green leaf pigment, chlorophyll, is a nitrogenous compound.

Nitrogen is most active in the young, tender parts of plant tissues, such as tips of shoots, buds, and opening leaves. If there's a deficiency, only the growing tips will function properly. Older cells may turn yellow, and old leaves may die and drop off.

PHOSPHORUS

Next on the analysis list of a fertilizer label is the percentage of phosphorus.

The mineral or clay particles that contain phosphorus ions

give them up reluctantly to the microscopic film (soil solution) that surrounds the particles. As the root tips grow into contact with the soil solution, they absorb phosphorus that the solution is holding in available form. This reduces the concentration of phosphorus ions in the soil solution around the root tips, and the phosphorus becomes insufficient to meet the plant's needs. Then, more phosphorus is released from the particle to the solution surrounding it, and the root takes it up.

The root grows on to fresh areas of soil solution, repeating the process. During periods of rapid growth, the phosphorus absorption and renewal cycle around a soil particle takes place constantly, if the soil is fertile. If the concentration of phosphorus in the soil solution is too low, or if the rate of renewal is too slow, plant growth is retarded.

Why phosphorus moves slowly. The phosphoric acid from fertilizer ionizes in the soil to form other phosphate compounds, some of which plants can use, some of which are so insoluble that plants cannot use them. This is called "fixation," and it is more of a problem in definitely acid soils than in neutral or alkaline soils. (In acid soil there is an abundance of certain iron and aluminum compounds that combine readily with common phosphate compounds, making the phosphorus insoluble and therefore unavailable.) If yours is an acid soil, you should raise your soil's available phosphorus level to a point where the fixing power has been satisfied and there are no longer many "hungry" minerals to combine with the phosphate ions.

The least effective ways of applying a fertilizer containing phosphorus are to broadcast and mix it lightly into the surface or to spray a solution on the soil surface. This allows maximum fixation to develop because, for every widely separated granule, there are many "hungry" minerals waiting to combine with the phosphorus and make it unavailable.

Best way to apply. The wisest thing acid soil gardeners can do is to concentrate the phosphates in a place where roots can get at them, where the drawing-and-replenishing cycle described above can take place over a long time.

In practical terms this means banding fertilizer beside seed rows—a few inches to one side and a few inches below the seed level (following label directions for amounts per foot of row). For existing trees and shrubs, try banding out around the dripline (far ends of the branches); or drill holes into the soil around the dripline and place the fertilizer in these holes.

When you plant a new tree or shrub, dig in superphosphate or a complete fertilizer that contains phosphorus as well as nitrogen and potash. Thoroughly mix as much as label directions will allow into what you estimate will be the root area for a few years to come.

What phosphorus does. Phosphorus is necessary for the process of photosynthesis and it provides the mechanism by which energy is transferred within a plant. It is present in all living tissue.

POTASSIUM

Usually, the last percentage listed in the label's analysis is potassium. It's said in different ways on different labels: "available or soluble potash," "water soluble potash," "water soluble potash from muriate or tankage."

Plants remove from the soil more potassium than any other nutrients except nitrogen and calcium.

Potassium in the soil exists in several forms. One form is soluble in water; other forms are insoluble; some are insoluble even in strong acids. Most of the natural soil potassium is not available to plants even though plants have been growing in the soil for years.

Little made available. About 1 per cent of the total soil potassium is an important reservoir. It's what is called exchangeable potassium. It may be derived from minerals or fertilizers or crop residues.

If the potassium is an exchangeable form, it is not soluble or free to move with soil water unless it is replaced or undergoes a slow weathering process. However, roots can pick up exchangeable potassium from the clay or humus particle without that element actually entering the soil solution.

When you add fertilizer containing soluble potassium to the soil, a transfer occurs from solution to exchangeable potassium. An equilibrium is re-established at a higher potassium level.

What potassium does. Potassium is essential to the life processes of a plant, including manufacture and movement of sugars and starch, and normal growth by cell division.

SULFUR, MAGNESIUM, CALCIUM

Some fertilizers contain these elements, others do not. Actually, it makes little difference; these elements, while important, are usually present in the soil in good supply. Also, calcium and sulfur get into the soil in other kinds of garden products: lime (calcium), lime-sulfur fungicides and soil conditioners (calcium and sulfur), gypsum (calcium and sulfur), superphosphate (some sulfur in addition to the phosphates), and soil sulfur used for acidifying alkaline soils.

Sulfur gets into soils in ways you'd never expect. Municipal water in many areas contain dissolved sulfur in forms that plants can use. Near industrial cities rain water often carries sulfur picked up from fumes in the atmosphere.

Both sulfur and calcium are contained in organic matter. Sulfur released in the decomposition declines in proportion to the decrease in release of nitrogen. You add great quantities of calcium every time you use lime to correct acidity of the soil.

What they do. Calcium is a highly essential plant nutrient. It plays a fundamental part in cell manufacture and growth. Most roots must have some calcium right at the growing tips.

In the cells of green leaves every chlorophyll molecule has an atom of magnesium as its central part.

Sulfur acts hand-in-hand with nitrogen in making new protoplasm for plant cells, and it is just as essential, but its deficiency in the soil is not so prevalent.

IRON, ZINC, MANGANESE

If a soil is quite alkaline, as some soils are in low-rainfall areas, plants may not be able to absorb enough iron, zinc, and manganese. If you live in such an area, you probably know of the need for these minor elements. Nurseries and garden stores sell products you can put on the soil or spray on the leaves.

Some such soil products are chelated, meaning that the iron, zinc, or manganese is in a form that should remain available to roots and not be susceptible to the fixing or locking that makes the native iron, zinc, or manganese unavailable.

HOW TO FEED A TREE

Springtime, when soil has warmed up, is a good time for feeding trees and large shrubs. The method you use should depend largely on your climate zone and the amount of water the tree has available. With sufficient water available to them, a tree's feeder roots will grow and take up nutrients. But if soil has been allowed to dry out in any of the areas where roots have been growing, roots there will stop functioning and die. No amount of soil fertilizer will help the tree until it has grown a new system of feeder roots—a long, slow process. Therefore, any feeding program must be coupled with a diligent watering program to be effective.

Root system will be extensive on regularly watered side, but may be sparse on opposite, unwatered side. Water all roots until they are growing actively, then fertilize.

FOUR METHODS

Root plug feeding. This very popular method works best in areas of moderate rainfall and mild climate. Fertilizer placed this way must have sufficient water to make it available to nearby roots, yet not so much as to leach it out of the root area.

Use an auger to drill holes in a circle just inside the drip line. Make holes 18 to 24 inches apart (the sandier the soil, the closer the holes, since follow-up watering in sandy soil will distribute nutrients *downward* quite rapidly but laterally not very far.) Don't drill down too far—just to the surface root zone.

Use a complete fertilizer, carefully following package directions as to the amount to be used and dividing by the number of holes you are going to fill. Before inserting in holes, mix the fertilizer with an equal amount of sand. Irrigate immediately and thoroughly; otherwise you'll burn the roots.

Liquid feeding. This is particularly appropriate in dry soil regions because the nutrients are in a form immediately available to the tree. A follow-up application in 2 months is advisable.

Home gardeners can use a hollow tube into which are inserted soluble fertilizer pellets, or venturi tube attachments for liquid concentrates; both kinds attach to the end of your garden hose. Insert the tube to a depth of about 2 feet; water pressure forces the solution out to the roots. Holes should be about 18 inches apart, just inside the drip line.

Surface feeding. This method is popular in heavy rainfall areas. You can apply fertilizer by surface spreading or by creating small depressions at regular intervals and filling with either liquid or dry fertilizer. However, you must water thoroughly when you apply either type (200 gallons of water is not too much). Remember, too, that surface plants under a tree will absorb some of the nutrient before it can reach the tree-root level.

Foliar feeding. Applied with a pressure spray, foliar fer-

Before feeding, use a spade to be sure there are feeder roots under drip line (outer edge of foliage). Feeder holes must be placed where roots are; roots take in nutrients through tiny hairs just behind the ends of the growing tips.

tilizer works best in regions of high humidity or as a supplemental source of food where root systems have been damaged. Time foliar feeding to take advantage of high humidity; the fertilizer will penetrate the leaves only as long as they are damp. Try to do it in late afternoon, evening, or on an overcast day, so midday sun will not dry out the leaves.

PROFESSIONAL HELP

If you have a number of large trees in your garden or you anticipate special problems with feeding, it is best to enlist the services of a local tree surgeon. He employs specialized equipment to handle large-scale and problem tree feeding and will set up a program geared to your particular garden.

Root plug feeding

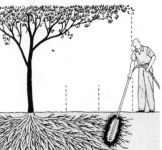

Liquid feeding

Surface feeding

Foliar feeding

FERTILIZING YOUR LAWN

No matter what kind of grass seed you use or how carefully you plant it (see pages 42 and 110), a lawn must be fed regularly if it is to thrive. A lawn, after all, consists not of a few dozen plants but *many thousands* of them, with root systems occupying all of the soil to a depth as far as 2 feet. These roots draw heavily on nutrients in the soil — especially nitrogen.

KINDS OF FERTILIZERS

You can use a slow-acting fertilizer or one of the fast-acting kinds.

Slow-acting fertilizers need be applied only once or twice a year. You can choose from many complete commercial fertilizers, organic types such as activated sewage sludge, or stabilized inorganics. Some products combine fertilizer with insecticide and/or weed killer.

Fast-acting fertilizers will begin to turn grass green in a matter of hours after application, but results will be only temporary unless you repeat the feeding every month or so. Many gardeners like to tie in this type of feeding with every second or third deep-soaking of their lawn, by applying liquid fertilizer with a hose-end applicator just prior to watering.

FERTILIZING TIPS

Timing is one of the important factors of lawn watering. Spring feeding is always essential in order to insure a strong, healthy lawn before summer's hot weather arrives. In mild climates, it is necessary to fertilize again in fall and winter if grass is to thrive during those seasons. A late fall feeding also shortens the dormant season of subtropical grasses by helping them to maintain their color longer. (You can also purchase a green dye for dormant subtropical grasses.)

It is wise to pay close heed to label directions. Do not, however, think of these directions as the one and only answer so far as timing is concerned. Learn to time applications so that *your* grass, in *your* soil and climate, receives a feeding whenever it begins to show the need. Loss of color is one obvious sign, another is loss of vigor, which you'll notice when the need for mowing becomes less frequent.

Nearly all fertilizers require thorough lawn watering following application.

Hand casting. *This works well if you do it in a slow, easy manner. Walk with wedding march cadence, make a semicircular throw with each step.*

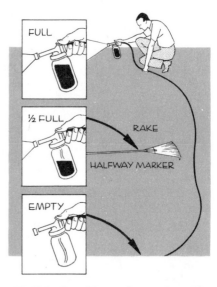

Liquid feeding. *Use a rake or other object to mark halfway point of area to be covered. Move fast enough to be there when the hose-attachment feeder is half empty, and at the other end when feeder is empty.*

Hopper spreader *makes the most uniform pattern. Two strips at each end give you room to shut off spreader, turn, open spreader, and start again. To avoid gap between runs, overlap previous run's wheel track slightly.*

Four common mistakes. *Left to right: (1) You can't turn an open hopper inside a previous turn and make a uniform pattern. Overlaps burn grass, and grass stays faded in gaps. (2) In foreground track you see what happens when you stop and start with the hopper open. Walking with an unsteady gait does same thing.* Concentrations burn grass or make it lumpy. (3) Strings represent wheel tracks on grass. If you run inside wheel down previous run's outside wheel track, you leave unfed gap. Even a good rain may not merge two swaths. (4) 180° turns cause erratic dispersal. One wheel drives sifter on inside; the other turns free.

CHAPTER 6

Directing Plant Growth

DOROTHY KRELL

STAKING AND TYING

Nothing is sadder than to see a beautiful young tree or a flowering plant beaten down by a sudden storm. You can avoid this disappointment if you follow proper staking procedures.

Some plants, particularly taller ones, obviously need staking if they are to stand up against the elements. Others, while they may not absolutely require staking, will not perform their best unless given proper support.

Always stake a plant securely and in as natural a position as possible; try to keep the stake and tie as unobtrusive as you can. Never make the tie too tight.

Adapt the staking technique to the plant's growth habit and the way it is used. Some plants, such as dahlias, tall delphiniums, lilies, and top-size gladiolus and tuberous begonias are usually staked individually. Multiple staking is the most efficient method for plants in rows, as in a cut flower garden; it also works well in group plantings.

Stake early to prevent damage to roots, to keep the plant straight, and to allow growth to adapt to and cover the stake and tie material.

Green-painted bamboo and redwood stakes are regular items at most nurseries. Also available are green plastic stakes with a wood-like texture. Ties hold more securely on rough wood than on smooth surfaces. In selecting ties, choose material that doesn't cut into stems.

The method depends on the plant . . .

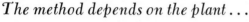

Delphiniums. *Stake must be long enough to support flower. Use ties that won't cut into the stalks or stems.*

Dahlia. *Stake is placed 2 inches away from tuber (left) at planting time; as plant grows (right), tie stem at intervals.*

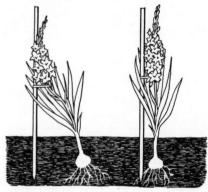

Gladiolus *at left grew crooked before it was staked. At right, stake was put in next to bulb at planting time.*

Wire device, *left, is good for carnations or other sprawling flowers. Right, same effect with stakes and twine.*

Figure-8 *tie is a useful trick. Secure loop tightly around stake, cross tie in center, circle plant stem loosely.*

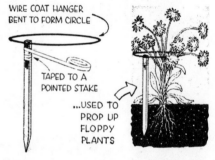

Wire coat hangers *are easy to make into supports for weak-stemmed plants—chrysanthemums, peonies, carnations.*

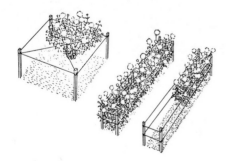

Plant at left *stands upright in triangle created by crisscrossing wire or twine. At right, plants supported in rows.*

Single stake *can support several plants. Place strong stake in center of informal group, tie plants to it individually.*

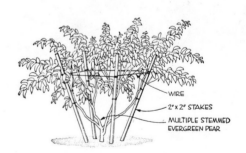

Multiple trunked *shrubs or small trees can be supported and trained on a frame of wood stakes and wire.*

ANCHORING TREES

To protect young trees against winter storms, use 3 guy wires attached to a rubber or plastic-covered tree tie.

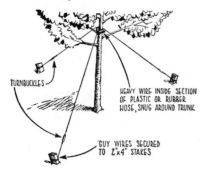

TURNBUCKLES

HEAVY WIRE INSIDE SECTION OF PLASTIC OR RUBBER HOSE, SNUG AROUND TRUNK

GUY WIRES SECURED TO 2"x4" STAKES

Anchor the wires to 2 by 4-inch stakes driven 2 feet into the ground. Set stakes, **making sure pull of the tree is against 4-inch side.** Use turnbuckles on the wires to keep them taut.

GROUND COVER "HAIRPINS"

Many ground covers will sprawl and spread out with no special training. Others, such as star jasmine (see sketch)

6" HAIRPIN MADE OUT OF 16 GA. GALVANIZED WIRE

will hug the ground better if you pin branches to the ground with 6-inch staples, starting when plants are young.

STORING STAKES

Unless you store stakes well, they have a way of getting underfoot. When plants die back, collect stakes in a wheelbarrow. Scrape and wash off the dirt, then let them dry before storing.

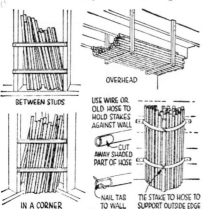

BETWEEN STUDS

OVERHEAD

IN A CORNER

USE WIRE OR OLD HOSE TO HOLD STAKES AGAINST WALL

CUT AWAY SHADED PART OF HOSE

NAIL TAB TO WALL

TIE STAKE TO HOSE TO SUPPORT OUTSIDE EDGE

Two ways to handle low growers...

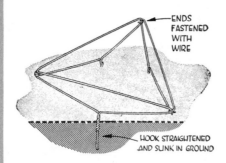

ENDS FASTENED WITH WIRE

HOOK STRAIGHTENED AND SUNK IN GROUND

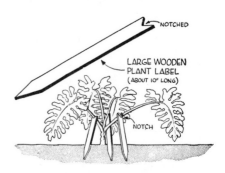

NOTCHED

LARGE WOODEN PLANT LABEL (ABOUT 10" LONG)

NOTCH

A triangle *of wire coat hangers makes a neat and stable support for low growing plants such as petunias and some kinds of fuchsias. Cut off the hooks of all hangers but one, which should be straightened out so that it can be pushed into the ground (close to the plant's crown). You can use the supports individually, in pairs on opposite sides of the plant, 3 in a triangle all around it, or 4 in a square.*

Flat wooden *plant labels—available in several sizes—can be notched to hold petioles or stems of sprawling plants. Good candidates include some kinds of azaleas, fuchsias, and camellias; certain large-leafed philodendrons. Supports are inconspicuous, especially if you dip them in green paint; they hold the plant more naturally than stakes and ties. Props can be moved as the plants grow.*

Training tomatoes in a cylinder...

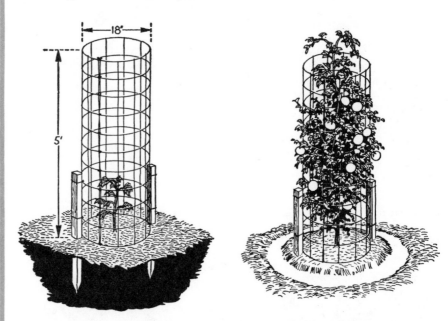

18"

5'

By nature, *tomato vines ramble over the ground. If the fruit is not to rot and be eaten by insects, it must be kept off the ground. This wire mesh frame cylinder, placed over plants while they are young, not only keeps the fruit healthy and easy to pick, but also allows you to spray, dust and cultivate around the plant easily. With it you can grow tomatoes in narrow beds; once filled with tomatoes, it is decorative enough for borders with flowering annuals. Use concrete reinforcing wire for the cylinder; it is rigid enough to be self-supporting. If you use wire with 6-inch mesh, you'll find that the tomatoes are easy to pick, and the vines easy to train. You can paint the cylinder to prevent rust and add to its attractiveness. Make a watering basin about 2 feet wide around each plant.*

PRUNING FUNDAMENTALS

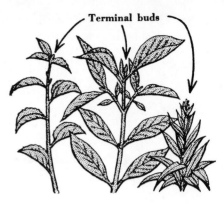

Of all the many gardening techniques, pruning stands alone as the most misunderstood—and most frequently neglected—of them all. The truth of the matter is that by understanding a few basic pruning fundamentals you can be well on your way to becoming a truly effective director of plant growth.

WHY IS PRUNING IMPORTANT?

General objectives of pruning have to do with modifying the growth of the plant to adjust it to the conditions of the garden. Some plants require considerable pruning, others may need little or none.

Specifically, you should prune to maintain plant health by cutting out dead, diseased, or injured wood; to control growth when an unshapely shrub or tree might result; and to increase the quality and yield of flowers or fruit.

IMPORTANCE OF TERMINAL BUDS

To understand the "why" of pruning, it is highly important that you learn about terminal buds. These are the growing buds on the ends of all branches and branchlets. During the season of active growth, these tip buds draw plant energy to themselves and grow, adding length to the stems. But if any growing terminal bud is cut or nipped off, growth ceases at that part of the plant and the growth energy which would have gone to that bud goes instead to other buds.

The flow of plant energy to a terminal bud is caused by hormones or auxins produced within the bud. When you remove the bud, one of the buds below will begin to produce auxin and will take over and draw plant energy to it.

The practical application of this lesson is that by pinching or pruning out buds you can make many plants—especially small ones—behave the way you want.

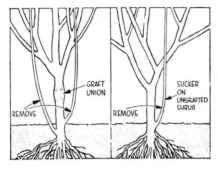

Suckers serve no practical purpose and should be removed as soon as they form. They are common on roses, lilacs.

Supposing you want a fuchsia plant to get denser. Pinch out all the terminal buds on every branch. This will force growth into all buds that are at the leaf stem bases along the stems. You will make perhaps two, three, or four new side branches where you had one lengthening branch before. When you make this happen all over the plant, you get all-over bushiness.

You make a young zinnia or chrysanthemum form several main stems instead of one by pinching out the tip of the single stem when the plant is young.

All seed-bearing plants *have important seed-bearing terminal buds. Here, left to right: plum, weigela, snapdragon.*

Supposing one main trunk begins to dominate an erect shrub or tree that is supposed to have many approximately equal-length main trunks. Cut back the terminal bud on the dominant trunk (if the resulting bushiness below the cut won't hurt the appearance) or cut out the dominant trunk altogether. One way or the other, you will be channelling growth energy into the terminal buds that were lagging.

Supposing a plant that should be growing vertically takes a notion to throw most of its growth into an errant side branch instead of the main vertical trunk or leader. Nip back the tip of the side branch (if you will accept the resulting bushiness at the tip) or cut it out.

WHERE TO MAKE CUTS

Whenever you approach a plant that you are going to prune for any reason—to take its flowers, to improve its shape, to make it bushier, or to make it more open—remember this: Make your cuts only above a bud, a small side branch,

Sometimes removal of a terminal bud means trouble . . .

If you cut runaways like these . . .

. . . the buds below the cut may respond like this

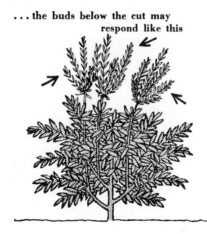

. . . Best plan, frequently, is to cut such runaways off at the base

Here is where to make your cuts . . .

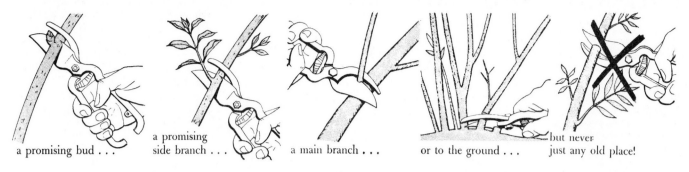

a promising bud . . .   a promising side branch . . .   a main branch . . .   or to the ground . . .   but never just any old place!

a main branch, or even the ground level (in which case the growing point is the roots).

Some smart person once coined a fine phrase for this advice and it's been picked up in horticultural literature a thousand times since: "Never leave a stub that you can hang your hat on." If it's a bud that you are cutting above, make sure you won't be able to hang

your hat on the stub after the bud elongates.

You see, among other things, a stem or branch is a sort of conveying tube. If you cut a branch some distance above its uppermost growing part, you leave nothing in the stub itself to maintain growth and there is no reason for water and nutrients to enter it. The stub is no longer a part of the plant's active

metabolism, so it withers and dies. Decay and insects can work into the plant through the dead stub.

If you have a choice of which bud or side branch to cut back to, choose the one that points in the direction you'd like new growth to take. And, if you, yourself, have no personal preference for the branch's direction, remember that generally it's better for the plant if

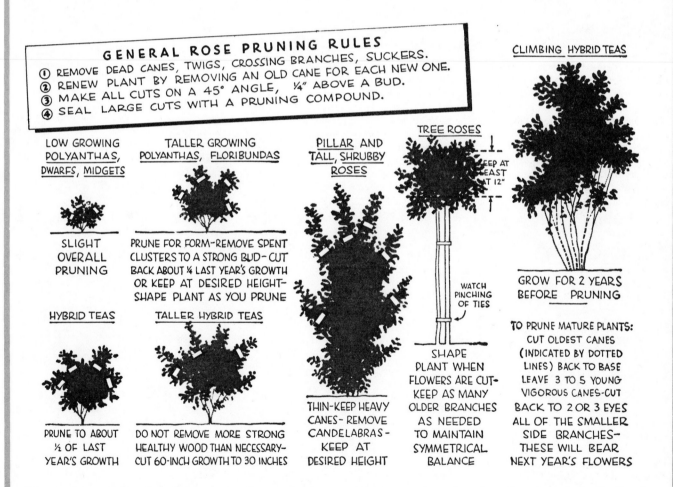

GENERAL ROSE PRUNING RULES
① REMOVE DEAD CANES, TWIGS, CROSSING BRANCHES, SUCKERS.
② RENEW PLANT BY REMOVING AN OLD CANE FOR EACH NEW ONE.
③ MAKE ALL CUTS ON A 45° ANGLE, ¼" ABOVE A BUD.
④ SEAL LARGE CUTS WITH A PRUNING COMPOUND.

CLIMBING HYBRID TEAS

LOW GROWING POLYANTHAS, DWARFS, MIDGETS

SLIGHT OVERALL PRUNING

TALLER GROWING POLYANTHAS, FLORIBUNDAS

PRUNE FOR FORM-REMOVE SPENT CLUSTERS TO A STRONG BUD- CUT BACK ABOUT ¼ LAST YEAR'S GROWTH OR KEEP AT DESIRED HEIGHT- SHAPE PLANT AS YOU PRUNE

PILLAR AND TALL, SHRUBBY ROSES

TREE ROSES

KEEP AT LEAST AT 12"

GROW FOR 2 YEARS BEFORE PRUNING

HYBRID TEAS

PRUNE TO ABOUT ½ OF LAST YEAR'S GROWTH

TALLER HYBRID TEAS

DO NOT REMOVE MORE STRONG HEALTHY WOOD THAN NECESSARY- CUT 60-INCH GROWTH TO 30 INCHES

THIN-KEEP HEAVY CANES- REMOVE CANDELABRAS - KEEP AT DESIRED HEIGHT

WATCH PINCHING OF TIES

SHAPE PLANT WHEN FLOWERS ARE CUT- KEEP AS MANY OLDER BRANCHES AS NEEDED TO MAINTAIN SYMMETRICAL BALANCE

TO PRUNE MATURE PLANTS: CUT OLDEST CANES (INDICATED BY DOTTED LINES) BACK TO BASE LEAVE 3 TO 5 YOUNG VIGOROUS CANES-CUT BACK TO 2 OR 3 EYES ALL OF THE SMALLER SIDE BRANCHES- THESE WILL BEAR NEXT YEAR'S FLOWERS

Different classes of roses *have their own pruning requirements. Prune when coldest weather is over and leaf buds are beginning* to swell. Annual pruning, shown here, is made simpler if you've kept roses picked and trimmed all year.

the new branch can grow toward an open space rather than toward another branch. Crossing branches are troublesome. They rub against each other and they spoil a plant's looks. You get them frequently enough by accident without encouraging them by pruning.

The only situation where pruning to a growing point does not apply is in shearing. In this case you are cutting such small, twiggy growth that the dead stubs are of no consequence.

HOW A PLANT WANTS TO GROW

A veteran gardener looks at and considers how a plant grows before he assists its growth by cutting or pinching.

It's the nature of some plants to grow long, erect, or gracefully arching branches with few or no side branches on them. You may wish to keep the plant that way, but, at the same time, make the ends more even or reduce crowding inside the plant. In that case, cut out the longest branches or the crowding branches (the ones that spoil the looks) right at their source. Don't tip them off even with the others. If you tip the too-long branch on a plant like

How to prune a fruit tree . . .

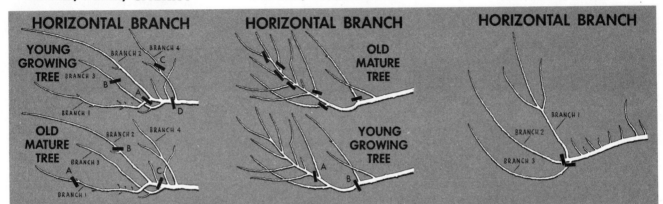

APPLE, PEAR, CHERRY

Young growing tree, *length being increased: Cut A removes branch 1, potentially weak. Branch 2 is left intact to grow in length. Cuts B, C subdue branches 3, 4, make branch 2 dominant. Mature tree, size being maintained: Cut A removes last season's growth, maintains length. Cut B subdues branch 2 in favor of branch 1. On older tree, Cut C would help stimulate replacement wood, not add to tree length.*

PEACH, NECTARINE

Mature tree: *Cuts marked here remove 2 out of every 3 side branches formed last year (rule for pruning these trees is to remove 2/3 of last year's growth). This is a thinning operation.* Young growing tree: *To shorten, cut at either A or B, depending on how much you want to shorten it. This is another way to remove 2/3 of last year's growth and at same time direct growth of the tree into selected branches.*

APRICOT, PLUM

Horizontal branch: *The two lower branches (2 and 3) should be removed, especially on apricot which tends to "come down" with age. These trees form fruit partly on spurs (short, stubby branches growing off main branch at right) and partly on last year's shoots (branches 1, 2, and 3). The spurs bear fruit over a period of several years. The shoots form spurs for next year the same year they bear the fruit.*

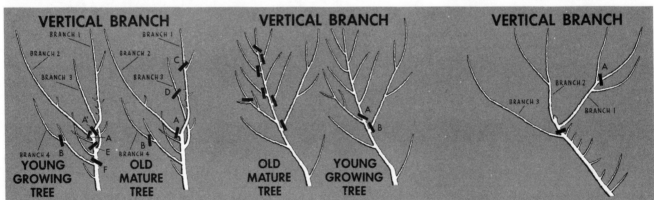

Young growing tree, *length being extended: Make a cut at A or A¹, depending on which direction you want growth to go. Remaining branch will become the leader. Cut B heads back branch 4 to help make branch 1 or 2 dominant.* Old mature tree, *size being maintained: All cuts made here —A, B, C, and D—are to hold back length. They leave no main branch intact, so none of them will dominate.*

Old mature tree: *Cuts shown here are primarily thinning-out cuts. They do not increase the branch length.* Young growing tree: *Here, as in the horizontal branch on the young tree above, cuts A and B will shorten branch and direct growth into selected branches that remain. These cuts would direct growth to the left. This kind of pruning is also good practice on very vigorous growing trees of any age.*

Vertical branch: *Cut at center of drawing would remove branches 1 and 2—typically the best cut to make here, especially if you want to send growth outward and make the tree more spreading. Or, instead of making that cut, you could cut at A to subdue branch 1 so branch 2 could maintain its advantage. Reducing the amount of wood in branches 1, 2, and 3 forces more growth into fewer buds.*

this, buds just beneath the tipping place may grow out, creating an ugly brush effect at the end of an otherwise graceful branch.

After a while, you come to know which plants will respond to a heading-back by making bushy growth beneath the cut and which ones won't.

As a matter of fact, you can train a tree or a shrub to grow almost any way you want if you watch how it grows naturally and learn (by trial and error if necessary) how it responds to pruning to buds at tips of branches, at side branches, or at base of branches.

Much of pruning is done to renew a plant within its allotted space. Left to its own devices, the plant might grow upward and outward forever, making its flowers or its new leaves farther out on the branch each year, getting twiggier and weaker. If you don't want this to happen, you cut back all of it or part of it at the end of its annual cycle. On just about all plants except those from which you want to pick fruit, the end of the flowering season is the end of the annual cycle and the time to prune.

PRUNING FRUIT TREES

The business of making a fruit tree grow to your eye's satisfaction, while still getting a good crop of fruit, is mostly a matter of knowing how the tree grows by nature, then pruning every year (when the tree is bare) to direct this natural growth as well as you can.

You can afford to be bold when you go about the job. A few wrong cuts can't kill a tree. The tree's growth in spring and summer will hide or correct most of the mistakes. It is usually better to prune and take the risk of making a few mistakes than not to prune at all.

The aim of all fruit tree pruning is to make or keep good tree structure and to force more growth into fewer buds, thereby making bigger fruit.

Peach and nectarine. These are the most vigorous growing fruit trees. This voluminous new growth of long, willowy shoots bears fruit the following

Use loppers *to remove branches bigger around than your thumb. For clean cut, hold so blade is closest to the trunk.*

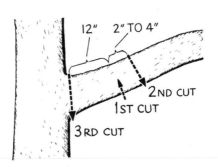

When removing *a large branch, make 3 cuts like this so that the bark won't tear when the limb falls.*

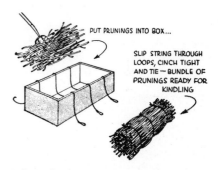

Cover cuts *over an inch in diameter with a commercial sealing compound to prevent rot and keep out disease.*

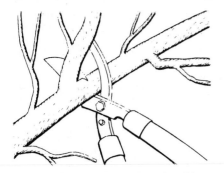

Pole tree-trimmer *helps you shape thin end branches. For big branches, you'll need a stepladder and a saw.*

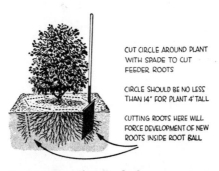

Root pruning, *if properly done, can sometimes shock shy-blooming shrub or tree into full flower production.*

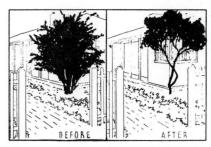

Salvaged prunings, *stored in this fashion, make excellent kindling wood. Let them dry out before storing them.*

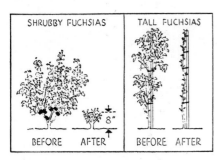

Fuchsias *bloom on new wood, require severe pruning after frost danger is past for maximum flower output.*

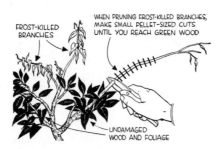

Wait *until frost danger is past and new growth is just beginning, then cut back dead branches to green wood.*

Overgrown shrubs *may be pruned to reveal pleasing lines hidden underneath excess branch growth.*

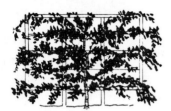
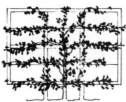

UNTRIMMED ESPALIER   **TRIMMED ESPALIER**

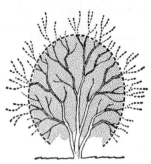

Untrimmed espaliered plants *(left) soon outgrow their trellis, then need severe pruning. Frequent light pinching of branch tips keeps espalier neat, trained to pattern.*

Evergreen flowering shrubs *should be pruned so that they retain their natural shape (left). Shearing back all branches the same distance produces "gumdrop" look (right).*

summer. The new growth bears only once. You should prune hard to encourage new growth; otherwise, fruit will be produced farther and farther out on the branches year by year.

Apricot and plum. These make almost as much growth as the peach, and need almost as much pruning. Although these trees grow fruit-producing shoots almost as abundantly as the peach, they also form fruit spurs (stubby fruit-bearing twigs up to 3 inches long). The spurs on apricot and Japanese plums grow very slightly each year and are usually productive for only about 3 to 5 years. By the time a spur carrying branch is that age, a new branch should be selected to replace the old one.

Slow growers. These include apple, pear, cherry, prune, and almond. Comparatively little new fruit-bearing wood is produced each year.

Pears, apples, and cherries grow so slowly that conventional pruning consists mostly of cutting out the dead, twiggy, and misplaced branches, and encouraging new branches. The fruits grow on long-lived spurs. Cut the vegetative growth back a little if it's getting away from you.

On almond trees, remove small branches to stimulate growth of new spurs and shoots, which bear the almonds.

POLLARDING, PLEACHING

Two pruning terms—*pollarding* and *pleaching*—are often used interchangeably, although they actually are distinctly different in techniques. *Pollard* means to shear the top of certain tall-growing trees so that the tree puts out a dense head of slender shoots rather than growing to full size. *Pleach* means to plait together, as forming a hedge or arbor; or to interweave branches.

True pollarding is rather brutal; the complete top is lopped off to 6 to 12 feet from ground level, resulting in stubby thick trunks and branches, unattractive new foliage tufts.

Modified pollarding is far more successful. Young trees are allowed to produce trunks to about 8 feet. Then, branches about the thickness of a man's wrist are cut to about 2 to 5 feet in length and allowed to callus over. In spring the tree produces slender wand-like branchlets; these leaf out to form a round, thick crown of foliage. Each year these slender branches are removed and the cuts callus over. With each pruning, knobs at ends of short branches get bigger.

Pleaching is practiced today chiefly to get a foliage canopy for high, light shade. You can pleach any tree that has tough branches and branchlets, but they must be supple enough to be bent and interwoven without breaking.

To get an arbor of pleached trees as

Pollarding and pleaching . . .

photographed below, build a sturdy framework of wood, angle iron, or galvanized pipe on which to train the trees. You will need as many vertical supports as trees, plus sufficient material to build a pergola-type trellis above the uprights and attached to them. You will also need 14 to 18-gage galvanized wire to string between the sections of the pergola.

Make vertical supports at least 9 to 15 feet high; and space them 6 to 8 feet apart. Set them in concrete for stability. Build the horizontal, overhead gridwork 3 by 3 feet. Within these squares string the wire—one wire lengthwise, one crosswise.

Plant and tie a tree to each vertical support. Remove side branches that develop along trunk. When foliage is abundant and reaches well into the overhead framework, you are ready to start training.

DARROW M. WATT

Pollarded *London plane tree in winter. Modified technique was used. Knobs at tips enlarge after each pruning.*

ELSA KNOLL

Pleached *plane trees on an angle iron frame, described in text above. Design: Thomas D. Church and Associates.*

KEEPING A "TIGHT REIN"

The secret to becoming an effective director of plant growth is the same as the age-old advice for developing a good golf swing: You have to follow-through.

Any of the four cultural tips shown on this page can be done in a matter of minutes—even a few seconds, perhaps—while strolling through your garden. None of them are absolutely essential to the health of the plant, but there are some plants that simply cannot perform their best without a "pinch here" or a "cutback there."

Pinching

If you are trying to shape young shrubs, trees, or vines, you'll find that pinching out new stem tips to force branching throughout the active growing season will save you from doing some heavy pruning in a season or two. Also, some annuals such as zinnia and snapdragon achieve better plant form if center bud is pinched from young plants.

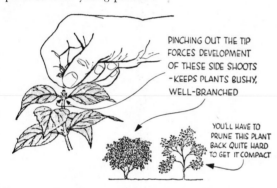

PINCHING OUT THE TIP FORCES DEVELOPMENT OF THESE SIDE SHOOTS – KEEPS PLANTS BUSHY, WELL-BRANCHED

YOU'LL HAVE TO PRUNE THIS PLANT BACK QUITE HARD TO GET IT COMPACT

You can nip *off tops of most plants with your fingers.*

Disbudding

Certain varieties of camellias, roses, and other shrubs produce more buds than they can mature properly. For this reason, many gardeners (especially those who enter flowers in shows) remove some of the buds so that the plant's energy can be concentrated in the remaining ones. Of course, some varieties are famed for their multiplicity of smaller or medium sized flowers; if this is the case, there is no point in disbudding.

SAVE

SAVE BOTH

SAVE

If you want fewer *but larger camellias, pinch off buds marked X. Some varieties thin buds naturally.*

Cutting back

Well established perennials (at least a year old) won't give a top performance next year unless you cut them back in summer, right after they bloom.

AFTER HELIANTHEMUM BLOOMS:

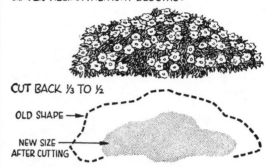

CUT BACK ⅓ TO ½

OLD SHAPE →

NEW SIZE AFTER CUTTING →

Be careful *not to cut perennials back too far.*

FADED FLOWERS AND STALKS...

NEATLY SHEARED BACK WITH HEDGE SHEARS

Use hedge shears *to trim soft-stemmed ground covers such as arabis, ajuga, nierembergia, yarrow.*

Thinning fruit

During the weeks when crops are beginning to develop on fruit trees, you should thin them. The remaining ones will then have space to mature fully.

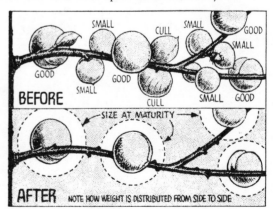

SMALL CULL SMALL GOOD

SMALL

GOOD

GOOD SMALL GOOD

BEFORE SMALL CULL SMALL GOOD

← SIZE AT MATURITY →

AFTER NOTE HOW WEIGHT IS DISTRIBUTED FROM SIDE TO SIDE

Leave 4 inches *between peaches (shown here) or nectarines, 6 to 8 inches between apples.*

TRAINING VINES

Before you select a vine for a specific landscape situation, you must be aware of how it will grow. Is it dense or rather open and airy? Will it stay within the confines of the area set aside for it? Is it deciduous or evergreen? Does it flower? Is it hardy? Will it be in scale with your garden?

Several hardy, long-lasting kinds are mentioned below. However, don't forget that there are many annual vines that grow readily from seed, such as morning glory, sweet pea, black-eyed Susan, scarlet runner bean, and moonflower.

Vines have "built-in" climbing devices . . .

Most vines come equipped with "built-in" devices that make climbing easy—twining stems, or tendrils or rootlets along the stems. Some have no way of holding on and merely ramble aimlessly unless you train and tie them. This does not necessarily mean that they are harder to manage. The persistent efficiency of twining stems or tendrils often causes a tangle and makes you wish they'd patiently wait for your assistance.

Here are some widely planted vines:

Hall's Japanese honeysuckle. Semi-evergreen to evergreen. Rapid growth to 35 feet. Needs heavy annual pruning. Fragrant flowers. Sun or part shade.

Virginia Creeper and Boston Ivy. Deciduous. Rapid growth to 100 feet. Foliage turns bright red in fall. Sun.

Grape. Deciduous. Rapid growth to 50 feet. Heavy, gnarled branches need strong support. Sun.

Wisteria. Deciduous. Rapid growth to 50 feet. Branches need strong support. Fragrant flowers in spring. Sun.

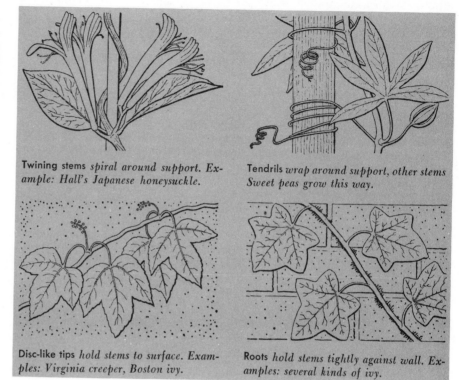

Twining stems *spiral around support. Example: Hall's Japanese honeysuckle.*

Tendrils *wrap around support, other stems Sweet peas grow this way.*

Disc-like tips *hold stems to surface. Examples: Virginia creeper, Boston ivy.*

Roots *hold stems tightly against wall. Examples: several kinds of ivy.*

Ways to train vines . . .

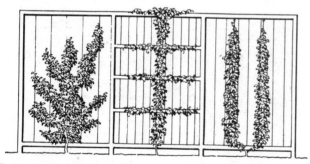

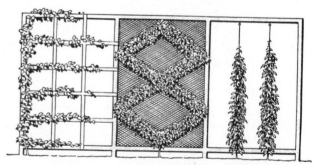

Train against fence, *make pattern with wood strips, wires.*

Screen planting *adds pattern, texture; provides privacy.*

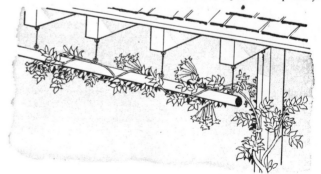

Left: *Hinged trellis permits painting.* **Center:** *wires and ties hold vines onto posts.* **Right:** *Dowel, held by wires, softens the eave line.*

Vine support . . . this hardware is useful . . .

The tie you use depends on the vine and the kind of structure that's supporting it.

For a lightweight vine, use soft twine, raffia, wide rubber bands, or plastic or reinforced paper ties. The ties can serve as an adjunct to the vine's own holding mechanism; when the ties weather and finally give way, the twining stems or tendrils will hold the vine firmly in place.

For heavy-stemmed vines, particularly those that have no device for holding on, use heavier, longer lasting materials such as pliable insulated wire, heavy rubber tree ties, sections of clothesline (woven cotton or plastic-covered), or strips of canvas.

Check ties from time to time; add new ones as needed.

Drill holes in masonry with a star or carbide-tip drill.

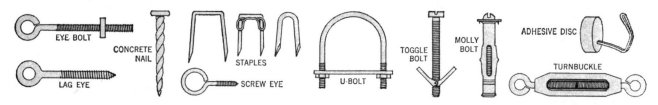

Special hardware *solves most of the problems involved in attaching vines and trellises to wood, masonry, and plaster walls.*

A hinged trellis makes sense . . .

An espalier or vine trained against a blank wall often is the answer to a landscaping problem, but can be troublesome when it's necessary to paint the wall.

The trellis shown here is hinged to its upright supports just above the ground. Hooks at the top hold it against the wall. To paint the house wall or fence, you merely unhook the

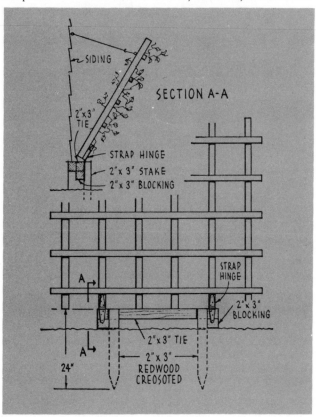

trellis and let it lean forward, supporting it at an angle with a stake. This prevents the trained plant from being uprooted, snapped off at its base, or otherwise injured.

After the paint has dried, the trellis is easily raised on the hinges to its upright position.

The design is by Architect Edgar W. Maybury.

Vines in containers . . .

Growing vines in containers is a particularly handy device for the gardener who has run out of space or perhaps is seeking a conversation piece for the patio. Wisteria, large flowered clematis, and ivy take especially well to container culture, as do the annual vines.

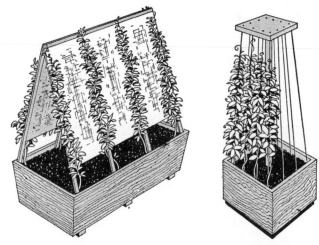

Trellised *container-grown vines give a quick, pleasing effect.*

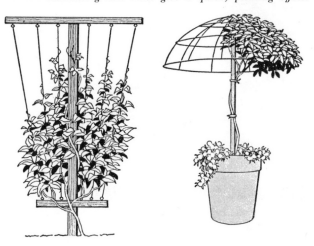

Left: *Vine support forms a baffle.* **Right:** *A wire frame "tree."*

ESPALIERING

Espaliering—the training of a plant into a definite pattern—is an exacting but rewarding art. Although many kinds of plants can be espaliered, with endless variation of technique, we have chosen a fruit tree (apple) for this sequence of drawings. Fruit trees are most often the subjects for espaliering, and for good reason: Espaliering exposes a maximum of branch surface to the sun, and therefore stimulates heavier flower and fruit production.

Apples, pears, apricots, cherries, and plums—about in that order—are favorite espalier subjects. Dwarf forms of all five are available, and are a good choice for smaller gardens.

If you live in a cool area, plant against a south wall or fence. In hot-summer regions, give plants an eastern exposure so reflected heat won't burn fruit.

Supports must be sturdy, because trees are heavy when loaded with fruit. Use posts of galvanized pipe or wood (4 by 4-inch), with 14-gage galvanized wire stretched tightly on turnbuckles. Leave 4 to 12 inches between trellis and wall for free air circulation and for working room.

Train the first pair of cordons (horizontal branches) to wire about 14 inches above the ground. Space other tiers about a foot apart.

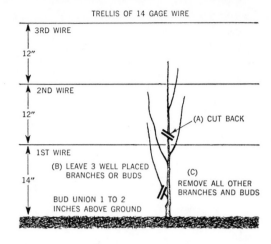

1 • *At planting time: Start immediately to train the carefully selected young tree. Two branches below first wire form first tier.*

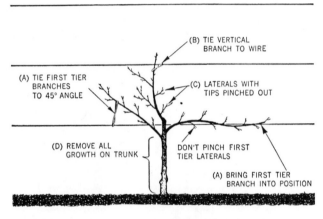

2 • *First growing season: Gradually bring first tier branches to horizontal position; straighten vertical branch. Hurriedly forcing branches into position may cause injury.*

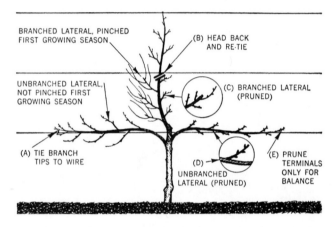

3 • *First dormant season. Heading back vertical branch below second wire and pruning laterals sets scene for second season. Second tier branches arise below cut (B).*

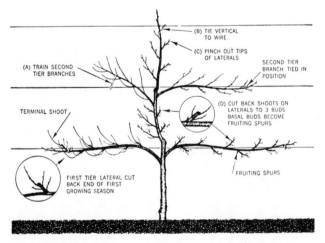

4 • *Second growing season: Train second tier branches as you did first tier during first growing season. Fruiting spurs now begin to form at base of all laterals below second tier. These spurs will produce some fruit next year.*

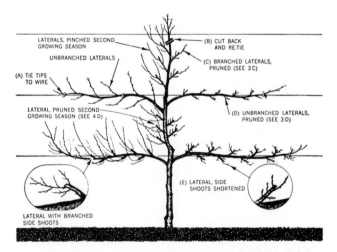

5 • *Second dormant season: Head back vertical branch below third wire. Prune second tier laterals as you did first tier during first dormant season. Follow similar training procedure in succeeding years, fitting tree to the space.*

CHAPTER 7

Summer Heat
and Winter Cold

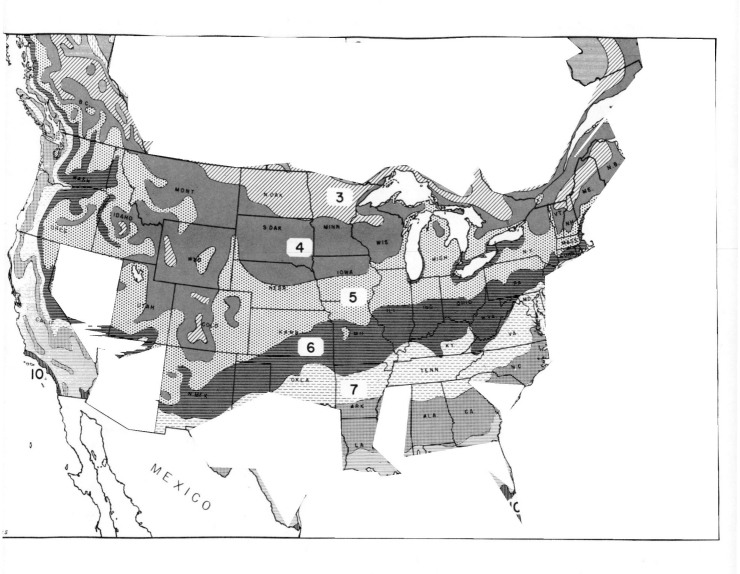

- If shade is scarce, make your own: pages 70 and 71
- Winter protection: pages 72 and 73
- Coldframes and hotbeds: pages 74 and 75
- Planting in hot weather: page 76

IF SHADE IS SCARCE . . .
YOU CAN MAKE YOUR OWN

The subject of shade in the garden is frequently ignored or misunderstood—particularly by the beginner. Perhaps he is fortunate enough to have mature shade trees on his property; or, if not, he may feel that concentrating on sun-loving plants is the obvious solution.

Actually, such an assumption is only partially correct. A basic knowledge of shade as it relates to garden plants will help any gardener in his quest for the oft-elusive green thumb.

"PORTABLE" SHADE

Seedlings and young transplants—even the sun-lovers—have a better chance of getting off to a good start if some temporary shade is provided. This is particularly true in hot-summer climates; however, in almost any region a sudden and unexpected surge of hot weather can damage young plants.

A portable shade device such as the ones shown on these two pages can be pressed into service at a moment's notice. It will protect foliage, keep roots cool, and conserve moisture. Even a few days of such protection can save you the frustration of watching some of your young transplants wither and die. When weather returns to normal and plants have become established, the shade device can be stored in the garage or some other out-of-the-way place.

A lath sunscreen should always be placed so the laths run north and south. (As the sun moves across the sky, strips of sun and shade move across the plants.) Also, since the sun is always a little to the south, let the south edge of the sunscreen extend beyond the plants to keep them all under shade.

A portable sunscreen makes it possible for gardeners to propagate their own seedlings, cuttings, and other young plants in a spot that might otherwise be too sunny and open.

PERMANENT SHADE

If you like to grow shade loving flowers such as tuberous begonias, cinerarias,

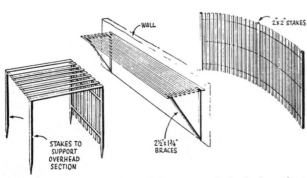

If the tree *you expected to shelter your shade loving plants hasn't filled out enough to do the job, erect a temporary overhead made with lath, bean poles, woven fencing, reed screen, or frames covered with saran or other cloth.*

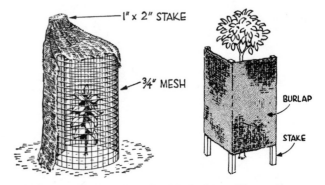

Left. *Wire cylinders draped with burlap will protect young plants from hot sun, drying winds, and animals.* Right. *Keeping bark green on trees planted the previous winter is a wise idea. Burlap cuts sun, allows ventilation.*

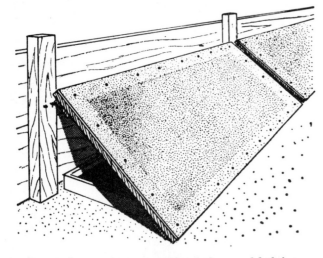

Seedlings in flats *can be protected by cloth-covered lath frames. Make frame of 1 by 4's, or use discarded window screen frames. Coldframe sash, available at some lumber and building supply dealers, is also good. Stretch cheesecloth or saran over frame; secure it with staples or tacks. Set frames against fence at angle; hold in place with hooks.*

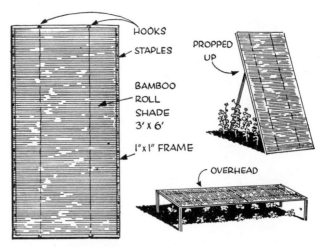

Bamboo roll shade *makes good cover for new seedlings. Build a frame of 1 by 1's to fit shade. At one end fasten hooks supplied with shade; attach shade to hooks and roll it to bottom of frame. Fasten loose end to frame before you prop it over new plantings. If you use this device on its side, use staples in order to keep the screen flat against the frame.*

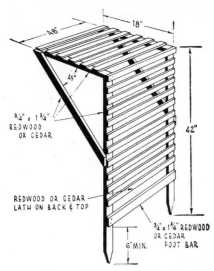

All-purpose *portable sunshade can be stuck in the ground where it is needed. Step on either side of heavy bottom rung to force pointed ends into ground.*

or cyclamen, you may want a shaded area where you can put them on display. There is no reason why a large but easily made shade structure cannot become a permanent part of your garden, provided it is well designed and soundly built.

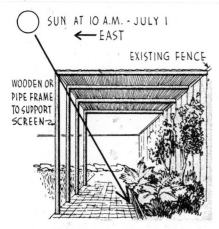

East-facing wall *needs a fairly deep overhang to halt sun by mid-morning.*

An east-facing structure is ideal, especially if you live in a hot-summer area. Your overhead, unless it is exceptionally deep, will get some morning sun; but from sunrise to 10 a.m., there is little heat accumulation. The plants will get enough light to keep the leaves green and functioning, yet they won't be burned.

A north-facing structure need not extend out very far. It should, however, be quite wide on the south side to protect against afternoon sun, unless you have a shade tree or a vertical screen on that side.

Easy-to-make plant screen . . .

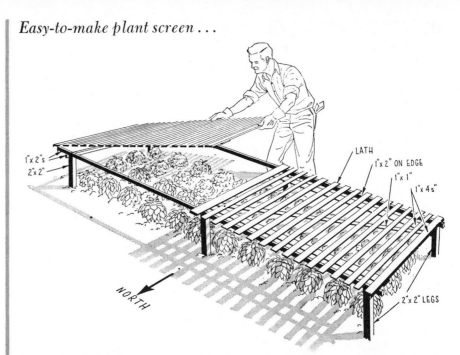

Lath screen and frame *(see photos below) moves easily to any part of the garden for temporary sun protection. It's also excellent for growing shade-loving plants that can be moved to a permanent display area when they come into full bloom.*

1. *Lay framework out by placing lengthwise pieces 6 inches in from ends of crosswise pieces. Nail together. Lay diagonal brace under crosspieces, nail it.*

2. *Post along the left side is to help you align the laths. Lay laths so they fit snugly together, starting at one end of the frame and working toward the other.*

3. *With aligning posts still in place, nail every other lath to stringers; this 6-foot screen required 22 nailed laths.*

BLAIR STAPP

4. *Remove loose laths. To stiffen frame, nail each lath to diagonal brace beneath. Mount finished screen over bed.*

WINTER PROTECTION

Protecting plants from cold weather is second nature to gardeners in regions where winter means snow and zero weather. Roses and other plants that can't take the cold are bundled up or buried under piles of leaves or straw. Container plants are moved to sheltered locations. Outside pipes are drained and water is turned off.

In mild-winter regions where frosts and occasional hard freezes occur, gardeners are not as likely to be winter-conscious. They grow many semi-hardy and tender plants that thrive in their climate, and quite frequently several winters will pass with no damage whatsoever. Then along comes a winter with temperatures dipping to just a few degrees lower; this is when unprotected plants can be killed.

A hard, ruinous frost seldom strikes like a bolt from the blue. You get warnings if you recognize them: There are almost always several nights of light frost—the kind that nips but doesn't kill—before you get a frost that really means business. This is fortunate. You can trace the pattern of danger in areas where plant foliage has been nipped, in the whitened stretches of lawn or bare earth, and know pretty well where frost will strike later on.

The most dangerous spots are stretches of open ground exposed to the sky on all sides, particularly to the *north* sky. Plants in hollows or in enclosed areas where cold air is held motionless are also in danger.

Regardless of what kind of shelter you use, keep soil damp around plants; damp soil holds and releases more heat than dry soil.

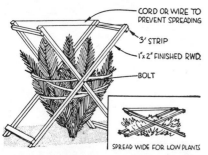

A cloth covering *goes over this portable, expandable frost shelter for tender plants. It folds flat for easy storage.*

Coldframe *(see page 74) protects seedlings or potted plants. Heat with cable if you live in a cold-winter region.*

Full-winter *frost protector might as well look nice. This one has Japanese design. Cover with cloth on cold nights.*

Cardboard box, *upside-down. Cut bottom on three sides to make lid. Open in day, close at night to retain day's heat.*

Bamboo *or other flexible stakes make frame for small "tent" of polyethylene plastic. Anchor plastic with rocks.*

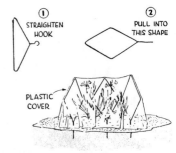

Wire coat hangers *make frame for plastic film tent. If wind is a problem, anchor with rocks as in sketch at left.*

Hotcap's *paraffin-treated cover allows some sun to penetrate soil in daytime. Trapped heat protects plant at night.*

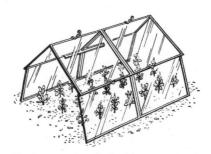

Cloches, *made of double-strength glass and available in several sizes, are set side-by-side to protect large area.*

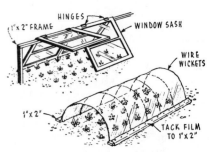

Two variations of cloche: *a tent of sash, a portable tunnel. Plastic film makes a good (and safe) substitute for glass.*

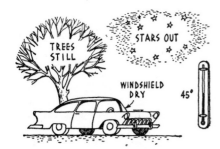

Expect *a humdinger of a frost in the morning when you notice these telltale signs at bedtime the evening before.*

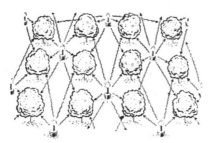

In a small orchard, *outdoor heaters can increase effective temperatures by radiation. Every side of tree should "see" a heater.*

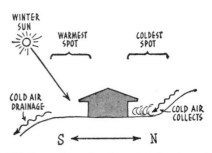

Hillside gardens *often have definite thermal belts and arctic regions. Illustration shows some of the main causes.*

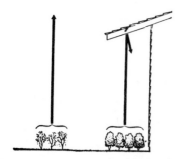

Plants under eaves *of house will often escape injury from freeze, while those a foot or two away suffer damage.*

An open overhead *framework can be converted into a weatherproof roof during winter by attaching plastic film.*

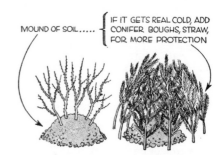

Canes and roots *of roses must be protected from freezing weather in cold-winter sections of the country.*

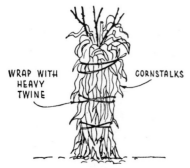

Canes *of climbing roses and other tall growers need protection such as this if they are to endure cold winters.*

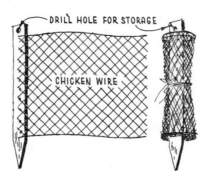

Another good way *to protect rose canes in very cold climates: Make a cylinder of chicken wire to fit around plant. Hold in*

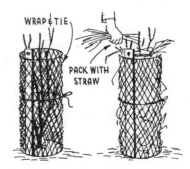

place with wooden stake; stuff with straw or other insulating material. To store, roll wire on stake, hang stake on a nail.

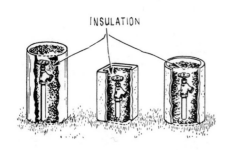

Hard freezes *can harm exposed faucets full of water. Cover with can, flue, or drain tile; fill with insulation.*

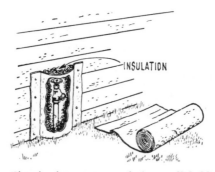

Sheath *of tar paper tacked to wall holds insulation of rock wool, glass fiber, peat moss, sawdust, or straw.*

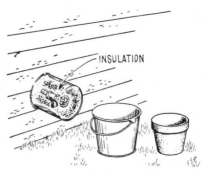

Gallon can *over faucet holds insulating material. You can also use a bucket or clay pot; or wrap with bandage.*

COLDFRAMES AND HOTBEDS

Experienced gardeners look upon a coldframe as an almost indispensable tool to successful year around gardening. A well built, well managed coldframe is almost as useful as a small greenhouse.

In milder climates, coldframes afford frost protection and air temperatures that keep plants growing right through the winter. In cold winter regions, they will do the same thing provided that an auxiliary heating system is provided. (A coldframe with auxiliary heating is known as a hotbed; where we use the term "coldframe" in this discussion, it can be assumed that we are referring to a hotbed if you live in a cold climate.)

A coldframe is useful for early sowing of summer annuals, protecting tender plants in winter, rooting cuttings faster, starting perennials from seed in summer, and growing many kinds of plants you wouldn't otherwise attempt to grow.

How can a structure as simple as a coldframe, basically four walls with a transparent roof, make this possible? It's easy to understand when you think of the coldframe as a controlled weather capsule in which temperature, humidity, and light are kept within the limits favorable for plant growth. Plants in a coldframe continue to grow even when outside temperatures fall below 45°, the point at which most growth stops.

The coldframe traps heat by admitting the short rays of the sun through its transparent roof of glass or plastic, and holding heat from the longer rays as they're re-radiated by the soil. In addition the cooling and drying effects of evaporation and wind are held to a minimum within this nearly airtight structure. The hotcap, a dome of heavy waxed paper used to protect tomatoes, melons, and other tender plants from late spring frosts, is one of the simplest and oldest plant protectors. It's a coldframe in principle, but without its versatility.

Hotcaps (see page 72) work on same principle as coldframes.

Since the coldframe is heated by the sun, point it toward that source. A southern exposure with a wall or fence along the north side for protection from chilling winds makes an ideal location. Be sure the site is well drained. If the wall or fence is painted a light color, it will reflect more light (and heat) down into the coldframe. A coat of white or silver paint on the inside walls of the frame also helps to reflect the light.

Equip your coldframe with a thermometer. Most temperate-zone plants can grow at temperatures between about 40° and 100°, with 85° the optimum. If it gets above 85° inside the frame, you can lower the reading by opening the sash to allow air circulation. But be sure to close the sash when temperatures start to fall (in the afternoon), to retain the heat that's been absorbed by the soil.

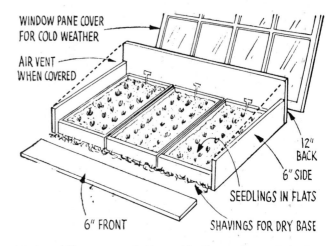

WINDOW PANE COVER FOR COLD WEATHER
AIR VENT WHEN COVERED
12" BACK
6" SIDE
SEEDLINGS IN FLATS
6" FRONT
SHAVINGS FOR DRY BASE

Simple coldframe uses 4 pieces of lumber, sash, wood shavings.

During a period of unseasonably warm weather, coat the glass with greenhouse shading (or whitewash)—this reflects sunlight and lowers the temperature.

To build a coldframe to fit your needs, consider the amount of space you have, the size of your garden, and how much you want to grow. You can build a portable coldframe in about an hour. A more conventional coldframe that answers most gardener's needs takes little more than a day to build.

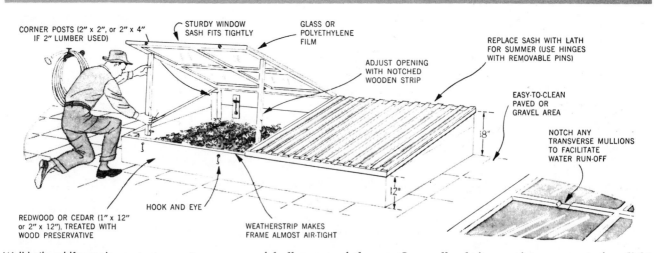

CORNER POSTS (2" x 2", or 2" x 4" IF 2" LUMBER USED)
STURDY WINDOW SASH FITS TIGHTLY
GLASS OR POLYETHYLENE FILM
ADJUST OPENING WITH NOTCHED WOODEN STRIP
REPLACE SASH WITH LATH FOR SUMMER (USE HINGES WITH REMOVABLE PINS)
EASY-TO-CLEAN PAVED OR GRAVEL AREA
NOTCH ANY TRANSVERSE MULLIONS TO FACILITATE WATER RUN-OFF
REDWOOD OR CEDAR (1" x 12" or 2" x 12"), TREATED WITH WOOD PRESERVATIVE
HOOK AND EYE
WEATHERSTRIP MAKES FRAME ALMOST AIR-TIGHT
8"
12"

Well-built coldframe is compact, easy to manage, useful all seasons of the year. Low walls admit a maximum amount of sunlight.

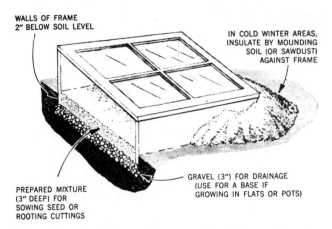

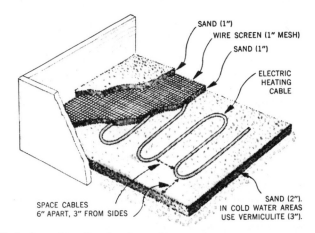

Cross-section *of coldframe shows gravel for drainage topped by a prepared mix. Air-tight walls are imbedded in soil.*

Hotbed *results when heating cables are added to coldframe; heating is a "must" if you live in a cold winter region.*

Several good, portable coldframes (some hea.ed) are available commercially.

You can make good use of materials that you have on hand. Scrap lumber of uniform thickness is suitable for constructing the walls if boards are carefully fitted to make the frame air-tight. Used windows or doors make ideal coldframe sash, or you can build a sturdy wood frame and cover with polyethylene film. New coldframe sash, 3 by 6 feet, is sold by most greenhouse supply firms. A new snap-together aluminum sash makes it easy to install polyethylene film and replace it when it is damaged.

In most cases, the size of the sash will determine the size of the coldframe. However, it's very convenient if flats, so useful for starting seeds and rooting cuttings, easily fit within the frame. Standard seed flats measure 14½ by 23½ inches and 18½ by 18½ inches.

In areas where night temperatures consistently drop below 32°, you can economically heat the frame with a buried heating cable or electric light bulbs. It's possible to operate either system manually, but an automatic control assures maximum efficiency. Even heat does wonders with hard-to-germinate seeds. Bottom heat from a buried heating cable is a great aid in rooting cuttings. Remember when you add heat to pay closer attention to watering since both soil moisture and humidity drop much faster.

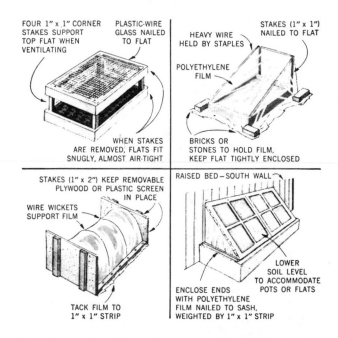

Variations *on the coldframe idea are useful, although they lack the convenience and efficiency of a conventional frame.*

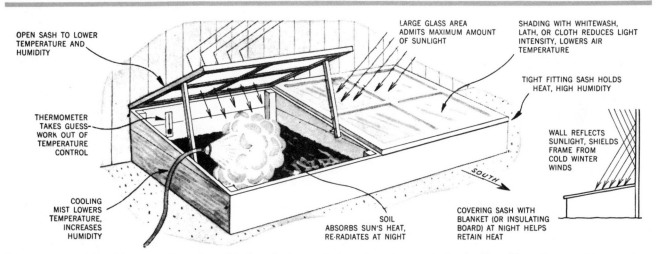

Keep temperatures *within range that's favorable for plant growth by using these controls. Avoid sudden changes of temperature.*

PLANTING IN HOT WEATHER

As mentioned in other sections of this book, spring and fall are by far the most popular planting seasons. This is not to say, however, that summer planting cannot be successfully undertaken.

Some gardeners—particularly those who have just moved into a brand new home—like to get their planting done right away. The fact that it happens to be summer shouldn't be a detriment; on the contrary, we know of many a new home owner who has spent all or a part of his summer vacation "greening up" his bare lot.

When you set out plants in the summer heat, you not only must observe the usual planting practices but must take extra steps to protect against high temperatures, low humidity, and drying winds.

Transplanting almost invariably puts a certain amount of stress on the plant, even under ideal weather and soil conditions. It is easy to see, therefore, why nursery grown plants that have been protected by windbreaks, lath, or cloth shade are likely to undergo considerable shock when moved directly into full sun, especially in hot weather. It is as though you were to dig up a plant that has grown in a cool region and then move it into a hot climate—it will have a hard time becoming acclimatized.

PLANT LATE IN DAY

Be sure your new plants don't suffer while they are awaiting planting; keep the roots and foliage moist and in the shade. Plant in the late afternoon or evening, or wait until an overcast day; this will give plants at least 15 hours or so to adjust to their new location before the heat comes on strong once again.

Here we show the steps for planting a shrub in hot weather. The same principles apply regardless of what you are planting, although bedding plants of course will not require such a large planting hole. For some ways you can make your own portable shade, see pages 70 and 71.

1. *Prepare planting hole in advance. Check drainage by running water into the hole; if water doesn't drain out within an hour or so, improve drainage (see page 6) or select another planting site.*

2. *Mix generous quantities of soil amendments with native soil. Moisten the mix (if you use peat moss, soak it before mixing by kneading in water with your hands; dry peat moss repels water).*

3. *Put some mix in hole. Bring plant from shady location where you've been storing it and set it in place. Handle with care to avoid breaking too much soil from around the root ball when planting.*

4. *Add remaining mix. Water thoroughly (note basin formed by rim of dirt). Prior to planting, you may want to treat root ball with one of the commercial products that speed root growth.*

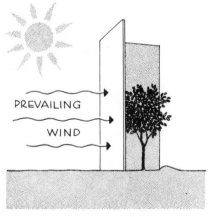

5. *Protect the shrub from heat and drying winds for several days with a portable structure of burlap, lath, or shade cloth. As an added precaution, apply anti-transpirant spray to foliage.*

PREVAILING

WIND

6. *Syringe foliage frequently with a fine mist spray. Apply a mulch over root area to cut down water loss from soil; mulch also increases humidity around plant as moisture slowly evaporates.*

CHAPTER 8

Controlling Pests and Diseases

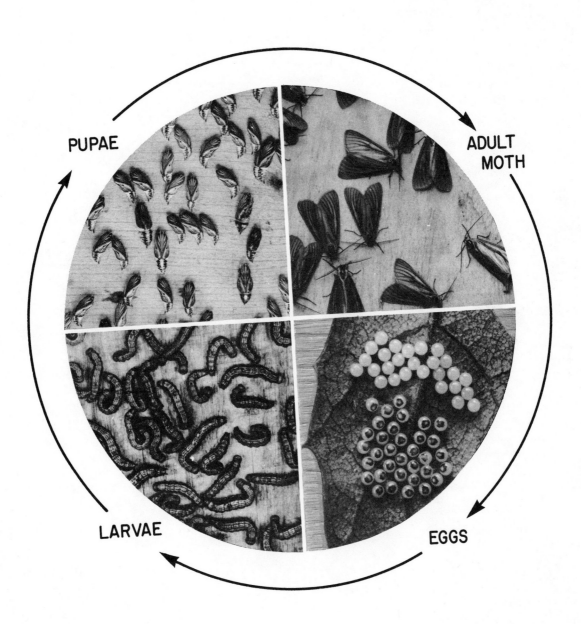

PUPAE

ADULT MOTH

LARVAE

EGGS

- Insect pests: pages 78 and 79
- Plant diseases: page 80
- Pest control techniques: page 81
- Moles, gophers, birds, deer: page 82

INSECT PESTS

The pests shown here are among common enemies found in home gardens. There are countless more, of course; however, once you become familiar with these representative kinds, it will be much simpler to understand the others. Below the discussion of each pest are recommended controls, keyed by number to the pesticide list in the far right-hand column. These chemicals are sometimes sold in "straight" formulations, but quite frequently they are combined with other insecticides and fungicides. They are listed numerically rather than in any probable order of effectiveness.

We have attempted to show and discuss not only the insect but the type of damage it does. Many pests feed at night, and the best way to be on guard against them is to recognize their symptoms. (If you want to see them in action, take a flashlight tour of your garden late at night.)

ANTS do not harm plants directly; however, they tend aphids, protect them from their enemies, carry them from plant to plant to secure honeydew.
CONTROL: 8, 10, 12

APHIDS are tiny insects — green, black, yellow, or pink. They weaken growth by sucking plant juices, and sometimes spread plant viruses. Ants tend them.
CONTROL: 1-10, 12, 15

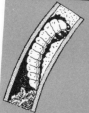
BEETLES, of which there are many kinds and sizes, chew leaves and young, tender bark. Hand-pick them (if you're not squeamish); kill grubs in soil.
CONTROL: 3, 7, 8, 12, 18

BORERS, the larvae of certain insects, burrow into stems and canes of roses, berry vines, fruit trees. Spray before the eggs hatch; prune off infested canes.
CONTROL: 7, 12, 16, 18

CATERPILLARS, larvae of butterflies and moths, are found in many shapes and sizes. They chew holes in leaves; some eat fruits, vegetables.
CONTROL: 2, 3, 7, 9, 10, 12, 18

CODLING MOTH is especially destructive to apples. The larvae chew their way right into apples. It takes several sprayings to insure control.
CONTROL: 7, 9, 12, 18

CUTWORMS are hairless caterpillars that feed on foliage, vegetables. Night-feeders hide in soil during day; another type lives on plant, feeds in daytime.
CONTROL: 7, 10, 12, 17

DIABROTICA, also known as the cucumber beetle, feeds not only on cucumbers but many other vegetables and flowering plants. Its larvae feed on roots.
CONTROL: 3, 7, 8, 12, 18

EARWIGS are voracious night feeders that eat leaves, flowers, other insects. During day they retreat to soil or any sheltered haven.
CONTROL: 7, 8, 10, 12, 14

FLIES (household variety) do no plant damage, but are bothersome pests. Good sanitation keeps them down. Poorly tended compost piles breed maggots.
CONTROL: 2, 3, 6, 10-12

GRASSHOPPERS feed on foliage, usually in late summer. Often found in warm, interior areas. Eggs, laid in soil, hatch following spring.
CONTROL: 7-10, 12

GRUBS are lawn pests which, like cutworms, live just beneath soil. Unlike cutworms, however, they feed on grass roots, not young grass blades.
CONTROL: 7, 12, 17

JAPANESE BEETLE is a bad actor; control is difficult. Adult beetles are especially harmful to roses, feeding on flowers and foliage.
CONTROL: 7, 8, 12

LAWN MOTH. Tan, 1-inch moths hover over grass and lay eggs on summer evenings. Larvae (sod webworm) live near soil surface, eat young grass at base.
CONTROL: 2, 3, 7, 10, 12, 17

LEAFHOPPERS are small, light green insects that suck juices from leaf's under side, resulting in a white stippling of upper side. Some spread plant virus.
CONTROL: 1-10, 12

LEAF MINERS are fly larvae that tunnel into leaves, producing a "mined" effect. Spray foliage to kill adults before they lay eggs.
CONTROL: 3-6, 8, 10, 12

LEAF ROLLERS are small caterpillars that wrap leaves around themselves for shelter and food while pupating in summer. They feed on leaves, new buds, fruit.
CONTROL: 7, 18

MEALYBUGS (aerial) are white sucking insects that develop in colonies at leaf and stem joints. Soil mealybugs attack plant roots.
CONTROL: 1, 5, 6, 8-10, 12, 15, 17 (for soil mealybugs only)

Warning. Many pesticides are highly poisonous to humans; follow label directions and use caution at all times. With edible crops, follow carefully the label instructions as to interval of time between application and harvest. Spray only if necessary (many insects are good for your garden, often preying on the real pests). Read page 81 carefully.

Read page 81 carefully.

MITES (red spider) are hard to see. Look for blotched leaves with silvery webbing on underside. One of the worst summer pests.

CONTROL: 4-6, 9, 10, 12, 15

MOSQUITOES do no harm to garden plants, but can make life miserable for the home gardener. A community effort may be needed for real control.

CONTROL: 2, 3, 7, 8, 10-12

NEMATODES are microscopic worms that sometimes attack roots, forming galls or root knots; plants wilt or die. Most active in sandy soils.

CONTROL: 19

OAK MOTH is a particular pest in coastal California, where larvae can strip trees of all leaves during heavy infestations (March to mid-June).

CONTROL: 7, 10

SCALE are small insects, usually covered by protective shells, that attach themselves to stems and leaf undersides where they suck plant juices.
CONTROL: 1, 4-10, 12, 15

SNAILS AND SLUGS (the latter have no shells) are not insects, but are bad pests. They chew foliage at night, hide during day, leave slimy trails.

CONTROL: 13

SOWBUGS, PILLBUGS. These pests, while an annoyance, feed more on decayed matter than on roots. Pillbug rolls into ball when disturbed.
CONTROL: 7, 13

SPITTLE BUGS attach themselves to stems, suck plant juices. They surround themselves with a protective froth, plainly visible. Common on strawberry.

CONTROL: 1, 4, 5, 7-10, 12, 18

THRIPS are very tiny insects that eat blossoms from inside, often causing partially opened buds; they also distort foliage by rasping surface cells.

CONTROL: 1-10, 12

WEEVILS of many types cause heavy plant damage. Adults hide during day, feed at night on leaves, fruit. Larvae live in soil, feed on roots.

CONTROL: 7, 8, 12, 18

WHITEFLIES are tiny sucking insects that feed on undersides of leaves. Stationary, scale-like nymphs do most damage. Leaves yellow and drop.

CONTROL: 1, 4-10, 12, 15

WIREWORMS are waxy, yellow, 1-inch worms that cut roots, bore into bulbs and plant stems, attack germinating seed. They grow into "click beetles."

CONTROL: 12, 18

Pesticides

1. Nicotine sulfate
2. Pyrethrum (pyrethrins)
3. Rotenone (cube)

These botanical poisons are for soft-bodied insects only. Lose killing power soon after spraying. Pyrethrum and Rotenone are popular for use in vegetable gardens. Nicotine sulfate is highly toxic to humans if taken internally.

4. Di-syston granules
5. Meta-systox-R
6. Cygon (dimethoate)

These are systemic insecticides with killing power that lasts for weeks. Plants absorb these materials into their sap system and kill sucking insects as they attempt to feed. Do not use on food crops; renders them toxic.

7. Sevin (carbaryl)

This carbamate is extremely effective on certain insects. Toxic to humans if used carelessly.

8. Malathion
9. Guthion
10. Dibrom
11. DDVP (dichlorvos)
12. Diazinon

A wide variety of pests are controlled by these organic phosphates. They kill mainly by contact action, and killing power may last for several days. Toxic to humans, especially if used in high concentration.

13. Metaldehyde
14. Sodium fluosilicate

These baits commonly consist of a stomach poison, an attractant, and a binding agent such as bran. They are toxic, so keep children and animals away from them.

15. Petroleum oils

"Smother" insects whose waxy coating or armor protects them from poisons. Safe to humans, but not always safe to plants, especially during summer; follow label directions carefully as to winter and summer dosages. Can be combined with certain other chemicals (acts as spreader).

16. Ethylene dichloride
17. Dichloroethyl ether

These fumigants attack the respiratory system of insects. Vapors and/or direct contact with these sprays smother or choke the insect. Toxic to humans if used carelessly.

18. Methoxychlor

The chlorinated hydrocarbons break down slowly, and retain their chemical potency, wherever nature may take them, for years. They are of the same chemical nature as DDT which is damaging to a number of higher organisms and is now found in varying quantities in soil, water, air, and organisms almost everywhere. Only methoxychlor breaks down rapidly and is considered safe for garden use.

19. Nematocides

Where Nematodes are a problem, you'll have to destroy them with a temporary soil sterilant such as Vapam or Mylone. These wipe out *all* insects and disease-causing organisms, but they also kill all plants; use only *before* planting. Toxic to humans if used carelessly.

PLANT DISEASES

Plants, like all living things, are subject to certain diseases and bacterial infections.

Below are listed some of the main ones, with recommended control. The surest way to minimize disease, however, is to use *preventive* control measures as follows:

1. Keep your garden free of weeds, fallen fruits, and flowers. If you find a diseased plant, pull it and burn it.

2. Spray or dust to control disease-spreading insects such as aphids, leafhoppers, mealy bugs, and thrips.

3. Wherever possible, buy disease-resistant seed strains.

4. Rotate annual plantings; diseases infecting a bed may bother some plants but not others.

5. Water and feed plants properly; a healthy plant has better resistance.

6. Set plants in exposures (sun or shade) that suit their needs. Don't set mildew-susceptible plants too close together; allow plenty of room for air circulation.

7. Start spray or dust programs early; badly infected plants are often beyond saving.

COMMON DISEASES

Powdery mildew. This fungus is particularly prevalent in dry areas where no rain falls in summer. There are many different kinds, most of which grow on a single kind of plant. Roses, zinnias, and certain vegetables are only a few that are susceptible. Fortunately, mildew is seldom fatal to plants, although it weakens them and makes them unsightly (see photos below).

Mildew generally starts under damp conditions in spring, but doesn't break out until the warm weather arrives. To prevent mildew, spray with copper oleate, sulfur, or phaltan. Karathane and actidione are effective eradicants.

Rust. These fungi produce small postules on leaves, which rupture and release red, brown, or yellow spores. Rust is most often associated with snapdragon, rose, chrysanthemum, carnation, hollyhock, and iris. Sprays containing zineb give good control. Merion and Kentucky blue grasses are also affected in some regions. Control is difficult; actidione is reported to give fair results.

Black spot. Most frequently associated with roses. Black spots appear on the leaves, which then turn yellow and fall. Ferbam, phaltan, and captan give good control.

Wilt. This fungus disease is fatal to asters, begonias, carnations, chrysanthemums, tomatoes, melons, and many other plants. Grow resistant varieties, rotate with non-susceptible crops, or—in extreme cases—use a soil fumigant. Pull and burn diseased plants.

Damping-off. Some soil fungi cause sprouting seeds to rot or kill young seedlings just after they emerge. The best control is to prevent its start by treating seeds with a fungicidal dust before planting, and/or starting them in a sterile medium such as vermiculite.

Peach leaf curl. This fungus disease of peach trees causes young leaves to thicken and curl as the spores germinate. Serious infections can cause much defoliation. Fortunately, the disease is easily controlled by spraying with ferbam, ziram, or a fixed copper fungicide before the buds begin to swell in spring.

Camellia petal blight. This fungus disease turns camellia petals an ugly brown. The best way to prevent it is to pick and destroy infected blooms, and not let any flowers or petals remain on the ground where they may produce spores that will infect the next season's blooms. It's also a good idea to renew your mulch beneath plants after each blooming season, hauling the old mulch away. PCNB, a fungicide sold under various trade names, is effective if applied to the soil before bloom season while buds are still tight.

Virus diseases. A number of virus diseases (mosaic, yellows, and others) are apt to strike almost any kind of plant. Much research is being done as to their causes and control, but to date there is little that the home gardener can do about them (fortunately, few home gardens are troubled by them to any great degree). Pull and burn any plant that has died for mysterious reasons. Keep aphids, leafhoppers, and other sucking insects under control, as they are known to be virus spreaders.

Powdery mildew on roses . . .

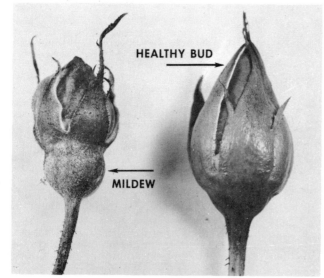

HEALTHY BUD

MILDEW

Buds infected *as badly as one on the left often fail to open.*

ROBERT ATKINSON

Healthy foliage *is at the left; badly mildewed leaves at right.*

PEST CONTROL TECHNIQUES

We cannot caution you enough on the use, handling, and storage of chemical sprays, dusts, and baits. These efficient weapons against garden pests and diseases have but one purpose—to kill. Although the poisons are intended for the pests, many can be very harmful to humans, especially to gardeners who won't take time to read the labels and to children who can't read and shouldn't be expected to know the dangers.

SAFETY RULES

1. Heed label cautions to the letter; 2. keep chemicals locked up when not in use; 3. keep children away from bottles and applicators while you're using them; 4. don't smoke while you spray; 5. spray when air is quiet; if there is some wind, spray with it, never against it; 6. don't spill material on your skin or clothing; 7. wash your hands, face, and other exposed areas immediately after you've finished spraying and have returned the chemicals to their proper shelf; 8. spray edible vegetables and fruits with great caution, heeding label precautions as to timing and residual toxicity.

It is a good idea to protect your hands with rubber gloves, and to wear a simple shield to protect your eyes and face (spray paint masks, sold by many paint stores, are excellent).

TECHNIQUES

When you spray is just as important as what kind of spray you are using. Follow label directions. Remember, too, that a regular spray *program* is far more effective than sporadic, hit-or-miss procedures.

Label directions are again to be stressed when it comes to measuring correct quantities of chemicals. Your regular spray equipment should include an old teaspoon and tablespoon for this exclusive use. Be precise; otherwise, you'll be wasting your time and money.

If you have a small garden, a spray program may not be necessary. Instead, an occasional bug-picking spree—done at night with a flashlight and a bucket or other container—can be not only rewarding but highly educational. Aphids and many other smaller insects can be "blasted" from plants with plain water, right from the hose nozzle. This should be done before mid-morning so that foliage will dry out quickly and not mildew.

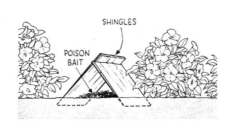

Many pests *seek shelter. This rig lures them; keeps children and pets out.*

To avoid *a possible tragic accident, store chemicals under lock and key.*

Some chemicals *kill mainly on contact. Be sure that you cover the entire plant.*

Chemicals *with long-lasting effects do some of their best work in the soil.*

Information on labels *is for your protection and knowledge; always heed.*

Formula *for dormant spray varies according to season; follow label instructions.*

Spray fungicides *with enough force to saturate cracks, folds of bark.*

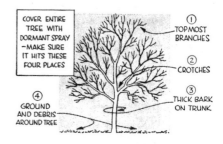

Dormant *spraying of deciduous trees, shrubs in winter pays off in spring.*

MOLES, GOPHERS, BIRDS, DEER

Plant damage by animals and birds can be a nuisance, particularly in rural sections and new homes in outlying areas. Here are some ways to protect your garden against some of the more common plant nibblers.

MOLES

Some kinds of moles feed mainly on bugs and worms; others would just as soon polish off a meal with some tulip bulbs, carrots, parsnips, potatoes, or other plant material. Regardless of their eating habits, their tunnels can raise hob with a home garden.

The presence of moles in your garden is readily detected by conical mounds of dirt pushed up from their main run 3 to 9 inches underground (moles, unlike gophers, don't open the tunnel). Another telltale sign is ridges of raised and cracked soil just above the shallow feeder runs.

The two most effective means of destroying moles are baiting and trapping.

If you use a commercial mole bait (many kinds are available), first probe for the main run with a broom handle or a similar long object. When you locate

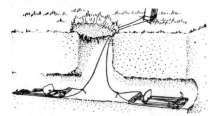

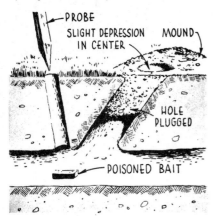

Macabee gopher trap is old favorite. Dig through mound to main tunnel; set trap and insert, business end first. String or wire ties, fastened to stake, prevent loss of trap, make it easy to retrieve.

Probe method, for inserting poison bait in tunnel. This is a gopher tunnel; same probing system works for moles.

it, you'll feel a sudden give as the rod breaks through into the tunnel. Drop in some bait, then gently close the probe hole to shut out the light.

Traps, of which there are several effective kinds, must be used with caution—particularly if you have small children or dogs whose curiosity might result in serious injury.

GOPHERS

Gophers are a problem in many regions, particularly in California and other parts of the West. They feed on plant roots and many kinds of bulbs, and are ruinous to lawns.

Gophers live in rather elaborate tunnel or burrow systems, usually from 6 to 18 inches underground. You can trap, poison, or gas them in these tunnels.

Usually, the first sign of a gopher's presence is a mound of fresh, finely pulverized earth on a lawn or flower bed. He expels the soil collected from his burrowing operations through short lateral runs which angle off the main run; he then closes the opening with loose dirt. Then you see only a crescent-shaped mound slightly depressed in the center.

Many gardeners who live in country places don't bother to trap or poison gophers, knowing that they can expect constant new invasions from the surrounding countryside. Instead, they place chicken wire at the bottom and sides of planting holes to protect plant roots from gophers and other subterranean marauders.

BIRDS

Birds, with their beauty and song, are to be treasured in any garden. To kill any birds other than starlings (they have no friends) is unthinkable.

In many regions, however, some precautions are necessary in order to protect young seedlings and transplants. Best protection is to fashion a shield of wire screen or cheesecloth that completely denies them access to the plants while they are becoming established.

Berries and certain fruit trees (notably cherries) present a greater problem. Ingenious new contrivances, often complex, are constantly being devised by home gardeners and orchardists. A long-time favorite method, usually partially effective, is to hang reflectors or fluttering objects from branches to distract and discourage the birds.

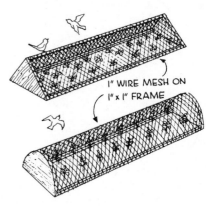

Portable bird protector made of scrap lumber, chicken wire or cheesecloth.

DEER

Deer are not, of course, as universal garden pests as birds, moles, and other forms of wildlife. However, if you live in a region populated by deer, you'll have a real problem on your hands unless you know how to discourage them.

For temporary control, commercial repellents are quite effective. Fencing is a better long-term control, however. If local building regulations prevent you from encircling your property with a tall fence and gate, you might try one of the fencing variations described below.

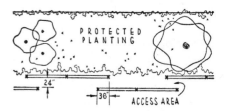

Six-foot-high baffles in staggered rows provide a maze that deer seem to avoid.

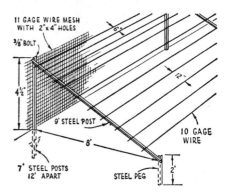

Low fence can be deer-proofed by building an outrigger that extends 8 feet out from the existing fence as shown here.

CHAPTER 9

Weeding Your Garden

BLAIR STAPP

HOW TO GET RID OF WEEDS

Weeds do well enough on their own; when you help them along with water and fertilizer, they really flourish. If not controlled, they can crowd out annuals and perennials and even small shrubs.

Chemical, mechanical, and hand methods of control are all effective if you start early and are persistent. The size of the area involved, the extent of the weed invasion, and the type of planting are the factors that should determine your plan of attack. Here are some suggestions on weed control and cultural practices that will keep the garden free of weeds.

HAND WEEDING

It's easy to get rid of shallow-rooted weeds: Just pull them up. If you're in the proper frame of mind, you'll derive a certain pleasure out of this. For the deep-rooted kinds, you'll need one of the many convenient weed-digging tools, such as an asparagus knife.

Several days before you start, water the area thoroughly, and then weed while the soil is still moist.

HOEING

Nothing can replace the hoe, the gardener's most useful tool for more than 4,000 years. Garden supply stores stock hoes of every size and shape; which is preferable depends on the type and condition of the soil you're working with and the particular job at hand. Narrow and pointed hoes are especially good for weeding around young bedding plants.

Advance toward the unhoed weeds as you go, rather than backing into them and trampling them under foot.

In areas where regrowth of persistent perennial weeds requires frequent hoeing, use a recommended chemical weed killer.

CHEMICAL WEED KILLERS

To list and describe all of the chemical weed killers available on nursery shelves these days would take many pages. Besides, there are newer and better ones being introduced constantly.

Rather than to cover them one by one, we shall break them down by classes from a standpoint of *how they work*. It is extremely important that you understand how each group gets the job done, so that you can relate it to your particular weed problem. Once you

Screwdriver *or ice pick is good tool for weeding between paving blocks.*

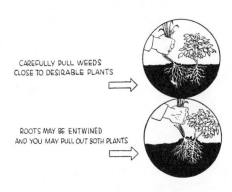

CAREFULLY PULL WEEDS CLOSE TO DESIRABLE PLANTS

ROOTS MAY BE ENTWINED AND YOU MAY PULL OUT BOTH PLANTS

Hand-pull *weeds that grow close to garden plants. Top circle shows the right method —pull up and away.*

know the kind you need, you should consult your nurseryman as to which specific chemical or brand he recommends.

Group 1: Weed killers used in established grass and dichondra lawns. Some kinds kill broad leafed weeds but do not harm grass. Some are seed and seedling killers that prevent growth of crabgrass. Newest are the non-selective chemicals used in low dosage to kill specific weeds or weedy grasses.

Group 2: Weed killers that knock down all vegetation. Since they kill only the plants or portions of plants actually touched by the weed killer, success depends on thorough coverage of all the weeds.

Group 3: Weed killers that *prevent* weed growth in garden plantings. These chemicals kill weed seeds as they sprout or after they are up—depending on the chemical and the use made of it. Sprinkling or rainfall carries them into the soil—don't spade them in.

Group 4: Weed killers that sterilize the soil. Use these chemicals where you want to prevent all plant growth for periods varying from months to years.

Group 5: Chemicals for complete soil clean-up. These chemicals usually function as a vapor or gas, which diffuses through the soil. They have a relatively short life in the soil—the treated area can be replanted within a month or less.

WAYS TO APPLY

You can use a watering can to apply weed killers on graveled walks and in paved areas where weeds grow up between stones or through cracks in the concrete. But this method has several shortcomings. When the can is full it is heavy and hard to pour. The solution is easily spilled. The limited capacity and coarse, wasteful spray make it necessary to refill the can repeatedly to cover a relatively small area. Perhaps the sprinkling can's best use is for quick

WILLIAM APLIN

Weeds *can be eliminated with one of the many and varied shaped hoes if attacked early, before going to seed. Your choice* *depends largely on personal preference. Here are three effective and popular kinds: regular, scuffle, and triangular.*

spot applications on fairly wide clumps or areas.

Tank sprayers seem to be the most satisfactory equipment when it comes to the application of weed killers. Their easily controlled, fine spray conserves the liquid, and the long wand makes it possible to reach in under shrubs and low branching trees. Keep the nozzle close to the ground to avoid drift.

Another type of sprayer is the device that fits on the end of your water hose. Best of such hose-end sprayers for weed killing is the kind equipped with a shut-off valve; the valve makes it easy to control the flow of chemical. Use of hose-end sprayers is limited to the application of materials that require a high dilution rate.

Caution. Wear gloves while mixing and applying solution. Apply on wind-free days to avoid drift onto valuable plants. Be sure that run-off won't wash down from high ground to the plants below, or damage your neighbor's plants along a fence line. Clearly label all weed-killing equipment and use it only for this purpose.

CULTURAL PRACTICES

Shade considerably reduces weed seed germination and weed growth. This is a good reason for encouraging shrubs to develop a wide foliage canopy. Gardeners often remove lower branches to make weeding and cultivating easier; but the increased sunlight then encourages weed seed germination and compounds the problem.

PREVENTING RECURRENCE

After you have cleared weeds from the flower bed or shrub border, apply an organic mulch 2 to 3 inches deep. This cuts off light from the soil surface and makes it impossible for most weed seeds to germinate. Peat moss, well-rotted manure (seed free), leafmold, composted ground bark, and composted

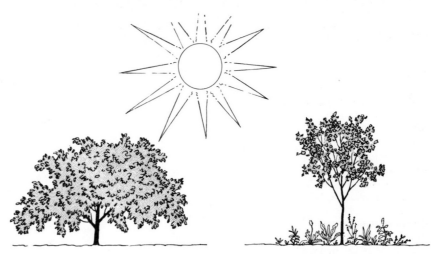

Spreading shrubs *shade the ground, allowing very few weeds to grow in their shadow.*

Weeds grow *between young ground cover shrubs; none after they have spread out.*

sawdust serve well for this purpose. Under a mulch weed seeds that may be present on the soil's surface are completely cut off from sunlight. Most seedlings die before they reach the surface and get the sunlight they need. The few that fight their way through the mulch are easily controlled chemically or with the hoe. Weed problems are virtually eliminated within a year or two if a uniform mulch is maintained over planting beds.

After *eliminating weed growth, cover open ground with an organic mulch.*

Watering can *gives coarse, hard to control spray; wastes time and materials.*

Tank sprayer *puts out fine spray for fast, thorough coverage; easy to control.*

Hose-end sprayer, *good for large areas. Drift is a problem in spot treatments.*

CRABGRASS

Crabgrass may or may not be the most universally hated of all the thousands of garden weeds. One thing for sure, however: It is the most *misunderstood* weed.

Many gardeners give the name "crabgrass" to grassy weeds that are not crabgrass (8 pretenders are shown in the sketches below). Not that anybody cares if you misname a weed! It's just that we don't like to think of your buying a crabgrass-killing chemical to apply to some weed that won't even be fazed by it. On the other hand, if your lawn really is infested with crabgrass (see the 2 kinds at right) we want to help you learn how and when to get rid of it.

Crabgrass is truly a wicked summer weed in hot-summer regions. In cool, or transitional areas, it is not of much importance.

Hand-pulling may be a perfectly good way of removing some weeds, but this is not true of crabgrass. Not only is it a difficult and tedious job well calculated to drive a man crazy; hand-grubbing actually pulls buried crabgrass seed into sprouting position.

CHEMICAL CONTROL

Chemical treatment differs, depending on the season.

In late winter or early spring, crabgrass seeds from last year that would otherwise sprout this year can be killed with a pre-emergence crabgrass control product containing any one of these ingredients: azac; balan (or benfin); betasan (or bensulide); dacthal, and Tupersan (siduron). For crabgrass in dichondra lawns, neburon is recommended.

In spring, when crabgrass seedlings have 2 to 4 leaves, kill with products containing any of the following: amine methyl arsonate, disodium methyl arsonate, calcium propyl arsonate or dalapon (spot-treated).

In summer, when crabgrass is in its full glory, certain chemicals can do the job: disodium methyl arsonate, amine methyl arsonate, calcium propyl arsonate, or dalapon (spot-treated). Two tricks that help to increase effectiveness are to water the lawn before application and to follow up with a second treatment 7 days later.

If your lawn has crabgrass this year, try mowing a little higher in future years. Grass cut at 1½ inches doesn't allow much crabgrass to get established.

Smooth crabgrass *is less common than hairy crabgrass (shown below). Both came to this country from Europe.*

Hairy crabgrass *looks like its name. Both this and the smooth type are pale green in summer, husky in appearance. They root at the lowermost joints in the stems.*

Don't confuse these pretenders with the real thing . . .

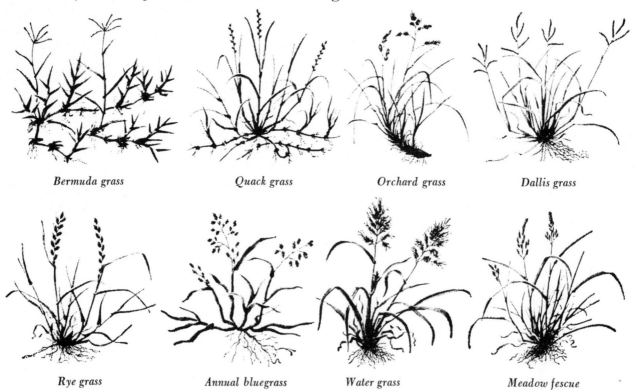

Bermuda grass	*Quack grass*	*Orchard grass*	*Dallis grass*
Rye grass	*Annual bluegrass*	*Water grass*	*Meadow fescue*

CHAPTER 10

Garden Tools and How to Use Them

DOROTHY KRELL

WHICH TOOL FOR WHICH JOB?

A new home owner, about to buy his first garden tools, may find the display of tools in nursery supply centers and hardware stores somewhat bewildering. Does gardening require such an arsenal? Which ones are necessary? What should you know about them?

If you follow your hunches, and buy the most familiar forms, shovel, rake, and hoe, you'll be right. But how about all the other tools offered? Actually, most of these were originally introduced to do specific agricultural jobs, but sometimes a home gardener found other functions for a specialized tool, or the manufacturer altered a tool's design to fit the home gardener's needs. The asparagus knife, for example, makes a dandy weeder, and the Warren hoe, originally designed for furrows and seeding operations, is now used more in home gardens for cultivating around shrubs.

DON'T BUY ALL TOOLS AT ONCE

It's a good idea to skip the specialized tools until you have gardened long enough to know your real needs. A hillside garden requires some tools you won't need if your garden is on the flat. Add to your collection as the need for special tools arises.

TOOLS CAN BE VERSATILE

Asking different gardeners for a list of tools you should buy won't prove much help. Tools are very personal pieces of equipment and all experienced gardeners have their favorites. We have asked a number of gardeners to evaluate some of the most widely used tools. Their answers show little unanimity but hint at the versatility of most tools. For instance, on the lawn rake: "The metal fan-shaped rake is ideal for collecting grass clippings . . . I like the light, easy surface touch of the bamboo rake . . . Give me the bamboo rake every time." Or on trowels: "An all-metal trowel will last forever . . . A trowel with a wood handle is less likely to raise blisters . . . My wood-handled trowel has lasted 22 years and is still going strong . . . If a trowel doesn't feel like part of your hand, throw it out."

In the accompanying notes and sketches, we make no attempt to judge whether a tool is good or bad. Your work habits, your plants, your strength, and your stature will determine which tools work most efficiently for you. The tools chosen for this survey are those most commonly used. We have not included any of the very specialized tools, or power tools, or lawn edgers and clippers.

It's not likely that any gardener would buy all the tools shown, for many perform the same function. However, when you buy garden tools, get the very best you can afford. A top quality product, if properly taken care of, will last you through most of your gardening years.

Don't buy any tool until you have checked it over thoroughly. Heft and swing the piece of equipment for weight and proper balance. A man-sized hoe may be just right for dad but too heavy for anyone else in the family. How about handle length? You may feel that a long-handled spade or fork is easier to wield. (It's a good idea to take along all the gardening members of the family when you're out buying garden tools.) Try the grip on all small hand tools. Get the one that "feels right" in your hand.

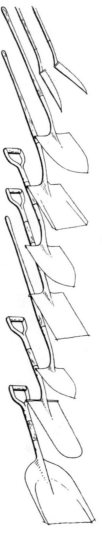

SHOVELS—

Long handle, round point. A versatile tool for digging, scooping, and shoveling. The round-point irrigation shovel (see sketch of two shovels at left) has a straighter shank, which gives it more strength and makes it better for digging planting holes or ditches with vertical sides.

Long handle, square point. For leveling areas for patios and walks, squaring off the bottoms of ditches, and shoveling snow. When shoveling dirt or gravel, this one is handy when you get toward the bottom of the pile.

D-handle shovels. For close-up jobs of moving soil, sand, gravel, and for picking up garden litter. Round point and square point models are available.

Square point spade. For edging and digging. This tool is easy to handle. You have a choice of a long handle or the shorter D-Handle. Always sharpen a spade before you use it.

Garden shovel. Somewhat smaller and lighter than the regular round point shovel. A convenient shovel for a woman gardener. Use it for digging, cultivating, and edging. It can be used with a chopping motion to break up earth clods.

Transplanting or balling spade. A favorite with experienced gardeners for balling shrubs and moving perennials.

Scoop shovel. For moving sawdust, manure, and other light materials. Serves as a garden dust pan for collecting litter.

SPADING FORKS—

Long handle spading fork. Long handle gives good leverage when you are working in hard soil. Breaks up adobe clods better than a spade. Buy the best quality fork; otherwise, tines may bend.

Short handle fork. You have a choice of a number of models. Tines range from 7 to 11 inches long. Weight also varies. Get the model that's right for you. Usually short handled spading forks work best in crowded planting beds or to lift clumps of perennials without damaging the tubers, rhizomes, or a plant's fleshy or thick matted root system.

Barn or manure fork. Not for spading, but for moving garden prunings, long weeds, manure, and other materials that hang together. It holds more than a hay fork. Also good for turning over layers of compost.

HOES—

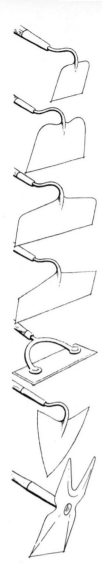

Garden hoes. There are hoes for just about every job. A hoe with a 2½-inch-wide blade for light jobs in narrow spots; an 8-inch-wide blade for drives and walks. The 6-inch-wide hoe is the most commonly used. A number of hoes have names that suggest their use: planter hoe, cotton hoe, square top onion hoe. The latter, also called a strawberry hoe, has a blade 7 inches wide and about 1¾ inches high; use around shallow rooted plants. To be effective, a hoe should be sharpened each time you take it into the garden. On hard cutting jobs, resharpen about every two hours.

Hoes with the conventional design of those sketched at left work best with a chopping action, the flat front edges cutting weeds off at ground level, or the sharp edges working like a small pick. Get a hoe that is light enough to be wielded for an hour or two at a time.

Scuffle hoe. A special hoe for the fast removal of weeds. You don't chop, but push the hoe ahead of you as if you were playing shuffleboard. It's a good tool for cutting the tops off annual weeds. (Perennial weeds need to be dug up.) This hoe works best on packed, level ground.

Warren hoe. For cultivating between plants or for making furrows. You make the furrow with the pointed end, seed, then turn the hoe over and use the "ears" to pull the soil over the seed.

Weeding hoe. Hoe on one side, weed puller on the other.

SPECIAL TOOLS—

Cultivators. Good for breaking up soil crust around plants. They won't qualify for deep spading. For best results combine chopping and pulling motions.

Weed and grass cutters. Weed cutter for rugged weeds and grasses in uncultivated garden areas. It removes top growth but not weed roots, unless you use blade as a chopper. Grass cutter is for help in cutting grass along the edge of a lawn. It is used like a golf club. Try various models for correct balance and weight.

Trowel. One of the most personal of all garden tools. Shop around until you get one that fits your hand, is well balanced, and light enough for your needs. A straight shank model is good for bulb planting. Drop shank is most popular.

Asparagus or dandelion weeders. For lifting out tap-rooted weeds in the garden and for weeding in such tight places as those between stepping stones in a path. These tools are useful, too, for small cultivating jobs.

Small hand cultivators and hoes. For close-up kneeling or sitting jobs or for planting on a hillside. The "business" end of these cultivators is the same shape and design as that of regular sized tools, but they are smaller, with palm sized handles.

Pruning saw. For use on branches larger in diameter than a broom handle. Curved saw on right operates on the draw stroke—hook the blade over the branch and pull the handle toward you. Straight pruning saws are also available.

SHEARS—

Pruning shears. Probably the most consistently used of all garden tools. Also available, in addition to anvil and hook-and-blade types, are special rose pruning shears and shears for cutting flowers. Buy a model that "feels good" in your hand.

Hedge shears. For shaping hedges, shrubs; cutting or shearing back perennials, ground covers, and faded flower heads. Some models have built-in shock absorbers. Hedge shears are not a substitute for pruning shears. They won't cut through thick stems or branches.

Lopping shears. Essential for pruning branches smaller in diameter than a broom handle. The long handle gives you greater cutting and reaching power. Handles are between 20 and 24 inches long. Some models have shock absorbers.

RAKES—

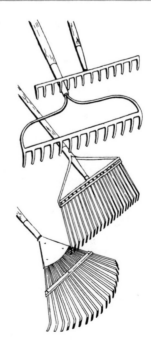

Level head rake. Flat top used to level seed beds and make seed furrows. It won't do the heavy work the bow rake will.

Metal bow rake. Good tool for leveling soil or gravel and collecting earth clods. The bow acts as a shock absorber, giving the rake a springy, resilient quality.

Lawn rake. Indispensable for raking lawns, leaves, paper, and other light matter on both paved and natural surfaces. You have a wide selection to choose from. Some are made of metal, others of bamboo; some are fan-shaped, others rectangular. On some models you can adjust the width of the raking face.

13 WAYS TO AVOID MONDAY MORNING GARDENER'S BACK

Many years ago, gardens were big, space was no problem, labor was cheap, and the trowel and the sprinkling can were the badges of genteel gardening. Pushing a lawnmower and turning ground with a spade were the ultimates in weekend exertion.

Today's home owners, on smaller lots, crowd much garden display into small places. Because paid help is so expensive, they do much of their own work with raised beds, big containers, and ambitious garden plantings and structures. They frequently use the station wagon as a truck. They put a lot of back work into many gardening weekends.

We show here a number of ways to take the "back" out of this back work: doing the job a different way or using garden adaptations of the simple machines you learned about in high school physics.

1· Lift with back straight

You've doubtless seen and heard instruction about the proper way to lift things—with your back vertical and the legs doing the lifting. Lift the wrong way and you can feel your back muscles complain. Nevertheless, the wrong way, hunched instead of erect, seems instinctive to many people, and the back strain that results is a primary cause of garden fatigue.

2· Use the inclined plane

This is such a simple supplier of mechanical advantage that a motivated monkey could probably arrange it. For suburban home owners, planks leading from station wagon tail-gate to the ground form the most frequently used inclined plane—for loading and unloading bales of peat moss, heavy sacks, large boxes.

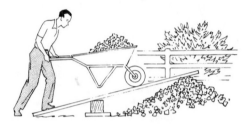

A ramp leading up the face of a dumping pile makes it easier to wheel a load up and make a tall conical heap.

3· Use the pulley

The physics textbooks say, "A single pulley merely produces a change in direction of force; a combination of pulleys secures a considerable mechanical advantage. The theoretical mechanical advantage is equal to the number of parallel ropes supporting the load." Here are ways we've seen pulley systems (blocks and tackles) used wisely.

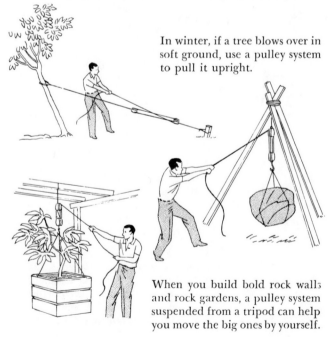

In winter, if a tree blows over in soft ground, use a pulley system to pull it upright.

When you build bold rock walls and rock gardens, a pulley system suspended from a tripod can help you move the big ones by yourself.

4· Use wheels whenever you can

Except in terraced and steeply stepped lots in hilly communities, we can't imagine running a garden without at least one kind of wheeled carrier. Unload, when possible, from the car directly to the wheeled conveyance, then push or pull it to the proper place.

Manufactured two-wheel garden carts are excellent for carrying big, bulky, or awkward loads. All weight is on the wheels. For gardens with narrow gates and paths, make your own—slim enough for your garden. Use a pair of bicycle wheels.

A child's large wagon is hard to beat as a garden carryall. All the weight is on the wheels; it's narrow enough to go through gates and down narrow paths.

Below. A platform on skate wheels or casters for edging and weeding along walks.

If a loaded wheelbarrow begins to tip, drop it! It may right itself; it may fall all the way over. But wrestling with it, especially if the load is heavy, can wrench your back badly.

Hand trucks are appearing as garden vehicles where owners go in for container plants. Extension of carrying lip helps. Shop for a hand truck with good wheel bearings, strong metal, stout joints.

5· Use the lever

In essence, you use the lever in one form or another all day long in the garden. But the lever in the classic sense, as illustrated below, could be used more often—especially to scale down a two-man moving job so one man can handle it. A long, stout crowbar, always a valuable implement around a garden, is best for this purpose.

To remove a stump, dig out around it as much as you can. Then, attach a chain around it, preferably taking advantage of any irregularities in the surface that give the chain a strong hold. Put jack on blocks under the chain. Hoist away to snap loose the remaining submerged portion of the stump.

To move a heavy object by yourself, take the weight on the fulcrum, swing lever in opposite direction from way you want object to go, take weight off fulcrum, reset, and repeat.

Jack can be used to push up and realign a leaning fence or structure before strengthening it in the new position.

6· Reduce friction

The hardest way to move any body over a surface is just to drag it. It's not the weight as much as the friction that makes your work difficult. Below are three ways to overcome most of the friction in moving garden objects.

Above. Use a series of parallel pipes or wooden rounds to roll a big box.

Right. Boards placed across lawn or soft ground make it easier to drag object.

Below. Shovel blade under a load supplies a smooth sliding surface, reduces friction.

7· Hydraulic action

If water is abundant enough and pressure great enough, you can use water pressure from the hose to do several jobs for you. Two are shown below. The hose-end sprayer, not shown, is an implement in which water pressure does work that you would otherwise have to supply with motor power or by pumping.

Stiff stream of water from the hose can blast leaves off grass or move many kinds of light debris from paved surfaces.

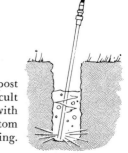

To make a device for blasting post holes and planting holes in difficult soil, use length of ½-inch pipe with hose-to-pipe fitting on top. Beat bottom end into a flattened or pointed opening.

8· To make soil diggable

Here are two suggestions for people who garden on clay or adobe soils. We've seen desperate landscape contractors turn to street-type jackhammers to break up dry adobe soil. But there is an easier way; just soak the ground four or five days before you dig. Do your digging in that magic interval between the too wet and the too dry stage.

A longer-range, more permanent way to make clay soil tillable: With a rotary tiller, blend in 4 inches of perlite, fine sand, pumice, or peat moss; or sawdust or fir bark plus nitrogen. This will last for seasons, perhaps years.

9· Store vertically or on a rack

It often makes sense to store long items—pipe, lumber, tools, stacks of flower pots, bales of peat moss, sacks of fertilizer—vertically rather than flat on the ground. They'll likely be easier to store, easier to pick up, and take up less room. For outdoor storage, off-ground placement offers few hiding places for insects, snakes, and rodents.

A wall rack for lumber and pipe makes easier storage (no stooping) and keeps the materials completely off the ground and away from moisture and insects.

10· Handle trash only once

After a day of tearing out old annuals, clipping hedges, and creating debris in other ways, plot your disposal plans before you start the clean-up. Dump the day's take into containers that you can take straight to the rubbish pile or directly into the car and then to the dump.

One good solution is to spread a big piece of canvas or tough plastic film and on it collect the day's garden debris. Roll it up and carry the bundle to the disposal spot.

The biggest cardboard boxes you can get at the market will take very large amounts of debris, and slide easily into the station wagon or car trunk if you drive to a dump. Boxes that held packaged paper napkins or facial tissues are fine for this purpose.

12· Move the ladder

The man in our illustration is not only courting "Monday morning gardener's back," he's also looking for a bandaged head. Granted, the apple just beyond always looks easy to reach. But you have to move the ladder anyhow so you might as well climb down and move it when you can no longer reach fruit with both feet squarely on the ladder steps.

If you are doing lots of work up in the air, get a second ladder and rig a plank between them. Make sure both ladders are solidly placed and that the plank is secure.

11· A king-size sweeping pan

A big time-waster and back-puller is the chore of gathering up leaves, clippings, and other refuse you've raked or swept into heaps in the garden. An easy way to get around it: Use a long-handled, king-size garden dustpan, as illustrated below.

Cut a 5-gallon can at a 45° angle up two sides and across top. Make smooth edges at top and sides around the opening by bending over edges.

13· Hire out the tough jobs

Be reasonable about your own labor. Hire the harder jobs done whenever you can. If there's an equipment rental agency in your community, rent machines by the hour or day to do jobs that can save you hours of hard labor. Some popular rental labor-savers are shown here.

Left. Electric hand saw for lumber. **Center.** Chain saw for cutting firewood. **Right.** Reciprocating saw for cutting firewood or pruning big branches.

Left. Power rotary tiller to cultivate soil to a fine tilth in small fraction of the time it would take you to do it by hand. **Right.** Some agencies even rent small power rollers for finishing soft paving. Avoids hand-tamping.

Left. Concrete mixer saves back, and blistering of hands. **Right.** Small tractor with blade in front, cutting-teeth in back for leveling and grading.

MAINTENANCE OF GARDEN EQUIPMENT

Garden tools, like any other equipment, will last longer and do a better job for you if they are properly maintained. Not that it is necessary to clean them and check them after each use—only one gardener in a thousand takes that kind of time and trouble. Just remember these three things: 1) Keep cutting tools sharp; 2) don't let tools rust; and 3) store them sensibly.

Hoes should be sharpened frequently with a file (see sketch below). This is a simple process that any gardener can accomplish in 5 minutes or less; the results are well worth the little trouble it takes, since the sharpness of the hoe dictates the amount of energy you must expend when you're using it.

Other cutting tools, such as lawnmowers, pruning shears, and saws, should be sharpened about once a year. If you don't have a sharpening wheel or other special equipment, check the yellow pages of your telephone book, under "Sharpening Service" for the names of shops in your region who can do this task for you. Cost is minimal compared to what you'd spend if you were to throw the tool away and buy a new one.

Before you put your garden tools away for the cold, rainy winter months, clean the rust from them with liquid rust cleaner (for especially stubborn jobs) or emery cloth. After cleaning, oil the working parts and put a light coating of cup grease over surfaces which are likely to rust. Drain fuel out of gasoline-powered tools. Clean strainers in lawn sprinklers.

Securely hang sharp tools out of the way—they can be dangerous. Store the lawnmower so the blades are away from foot traffic.

Most garden tools are hung, from one end or the other, in a rather standard fashion by means of nails, cup hooks, lag screws, or spring clips. Real satisfaction, however, comes from devising new and better ways to hang the garden hose. The sketch below shows 3 good examples; for the home inventor, however, these ideas will just be points of departure.

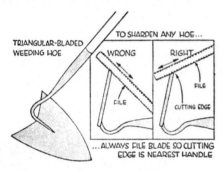

Right way *to file a hoe is easy way. Hold by handle; file away from you.*

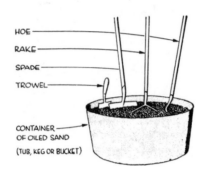

Oiled sand *works 2 ways; sand is abrasive for cleaning; oil preserves metal.*

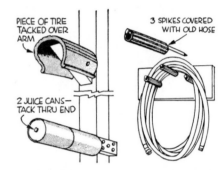

Methods *for hanging hose have one thing in common: they prevent sharp kinks.*

LAWN MOWING

The best and easiest time to mow any lawn is when it is dry—preferably in the later, cooler part of the day. Some gardeners, however, like to mow in the morning when they feel most energetic. There's nothing wrong with this, but first you must knock the dew from grass blades so they won't mash under the mower wheels, stick to the cutting blades, and slither under the mower. (*Never mow if ground below is soaked—you'll get wheel ruts.*)

Mow frequently—once a week is best for most grasses that are kept well fed. The short clippings need not be caught; they'll work into the soil and add organic matter.

If the grass does get long and shaggy, you'll have to catch the clippings or they'll pack down and smother the lawn. Rake the lawn first (see sketch below), to remove debris and pull up matted runners.

How close to the ground you mow depends on what kind of grass you have (see examples on page 110).

Other ways *to knock off dew: drag lawn with burlap or back of steel rake.*

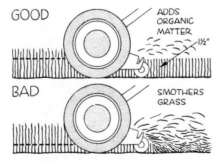

If you cut *your lawn often, you won't have to rake or catch the clippings.*

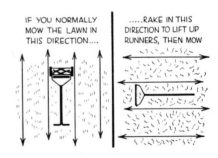

Before mowing *long grass, rake in opposite direction you intend to mow.*

CHAPTER 11

Basic Garden Plants

GLENN CHRISTIANSEN

- Shrubs: pages 96 and 97
- Trees: pages 98 and 99
- Perennials: pages 100 and 101
- Annuals: pages 102 and 103
- Bulbs: pages 104 to 107
- Roses: pages 108 and 109
- Lawn grasses: page 10
- Keeping cut flowers fresh: page 110

SHRUBS

Shrubs, along with trees (see page 98), form the basic framework of a garden. Other flowers may come and go, but once you put in these woody, vigorous plants you can look forward to enjoying them for many years.

There are shrubs—mostly hardy but sometimes tender—for almost any use imaginable. Most will do well in sun or part shade, but there is considerable variation depending on climate and variety. Generally speaking, the best shrubs for permanent landscaping are those which grow quite slowly but, once established, maintain their character year after year. Fast growers may overpower the garden unless kept in bounds by constant pruning and attention.

Never judge a shrub strictly by its flowers—or even its lack of them. Look for form and foliage. Let perennials, annuals, and bulbs be your pawns for adding color embellishments to your basic planting scheme wherever needed.

Some shrubs, of course, are real "show-stoppers" when it comes to flowers. Roses, for example, are widely grown and are universally admired for their beauty of bloom (they are described separately, on pages 108 and 109). Camellias, rhododendrons, azaleas, and fuchsias all are treasured for their magnificence of bloom in the milder sections of the country where they are most commonly grown. All make handsome container subjects—as do many other shrubs, for that matter.

The photographs show just a few of the hundreds of excellent shrubs you can choose from. (Evergreen and deciduous types are denoted by a parenthesized "E" or "D".)

DARROW M. WATT
Aucuba. *(E.) Plain, variegated kinds.*

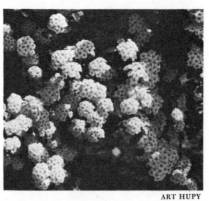
JOHN ROBINSON
Azalea. *(E. or D.) Many good types.*

JEANNETTE GROSSMAN
Beauty bush. *(D.) Pastel pink flowers.*

Boxwood. *(E.) Trims easily; good hedge.*

ART HUPY
Bridal wreath. *(D.) Tall, spreading.*

DARROW M. WATT
Camellia. *(E.) Superb blooms, foliage.*

JEANNETTE GROSSMAN
Daphne. *(E.) Tiny, fragrant flowers.*

ROBERT COX
English laurel. *(E.) Tall, fast grower.*

ART HUPY
Fatsia japonica. *(E.) Big, dramatic.*

Fuchsia. *(D.) For cool coastal areas.*

KASSLER STUDIOS

Gardenia. *(E.) Needs warm climate.*

RICHARD DAWSON

Holly. *(E.) Shiny leaves, red berries.*

Hydrangea. *(D.) Large flower clusters.*

ERNEST BRAUN

Irish heath. *(E.) Prefers a rich soil.*

DARROW M. WATT

Japanese privet. *(E.) Glossy foliage.*

CHAS. R. PEARSON

Juniper. *(E.) Many forms, varieties.*

GLENN CHRISTIANSEN

Lilac. *(D.) Graceful, fragrant favorite.*

BLAIR STAPP

Pieris. *(E.) Interesting all year long.*

Pyracantha. *(E.) Clusters of berries.*

DARROW M. WATT

Rhododendron. *(E.) "Trumpet" flowers.*

DARROW M. WATT

Rose. *(D.) Magnificent with proper care.*

TREES

Selecting a tree for your garden calls for considerable thought. First you must decide just what function you want the tree to serve. Should it provide shade, serve as a screen or windbreak, dominate a small or large garden area? How tall and broad should it grow? How soon do you want it to reach that size? Do you want an evergreen or a deciduous tree? What are its cultural requirements and winter hardiness? Will it fit in with the rest of your plantings and the surrounding environment?

Two of the most important factors to know when choosing a tree are the height it will ultimately reach, and how fast it will grow to that height. Fast growing trees that reach 50 feet or more in height should be selected with caution. The impatience of the new home owner to have good-sized trees in a hurry can lead to pitfalls. You cannot easily keep a 50-foot tree to a modest 20 feet; the fast, tall grower can quickly get too large for small properties. Such trees often cause concern because of shallow, invasive root systems or brittle, easily broken branches. Gardening under trees that drop great quantities of leaves is often difficult, too.

The first and strongest impulse is to choose trees we know and like. There are, for every person, certain trees that have emotional ties. We remember trees we loved in childhood—generally very large shade trees. If the trees you love will solve the practical problems of sun and wind, there could be no wiser choice.

On the facing page, we show just a few of the many hundreds of trees that can be grown in home gardens. Not all of the examples are grown in all sections of the country; however, if a tree you like is not available, your nurseryman may be able to recommend one with similar characteristics.

LARGE SHADE TREE

Ideally, a large shade tree should permit a lawn beneath it, should give a high foliage canopy, and should provide some shade in the second or third year after planting.

No matter what large tree you choose, don't expect it to be free of certain shortcomings. The pessimistic expert considers maples too large and too greedy of root, the ginkgo too slow and erratic, the elm too prone to disease. However, if you want one great tree in your garden, size and invasive root systems must be considered minor drawbacks when you consider the magnificence of the tree itself.

MEDIUM OR SMALL SHADE TREE

This should be a well behaved small tree, giving a minimum litter throughout the year. It should be fairly trustworthy as to size. It should give shade but not dominate the garden. You should be able to walk under it without doing a lot of difficult pruning to get this headroom.

The smaller the tree the greater variety you have to choose from. Direct growth of the tree into the form you want by pinching out tips of unwanted growth at low levels. Remove lower branches in the third or fourth year when the head of the tree is large enough to take over growth.

SUN, WIND, AND PRIVACY SCREEN

A tree with a low branching or weeping tendency is preferred to one that will grow a clean trunk. The wind screen should be 12 feet or higher, and works best if it filters rather than blocks the wind. Many gardeners grow screen trees close together in a row, and top them at the desired height.

In mild climate areas of the West, the medium-sized eucalypts make exceptionally fine screen trees.

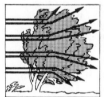

To save evergreens *from wind damage, thin branches to "put holes in the sail."*

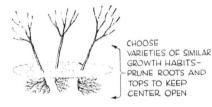

Planting *fruit trees in multiples makes a great deal of sense in the small home*

garden. *You can plant several varieties and spread out your fruit harvest.*

Soil *shouldn't be heaped around trunk of existing tree. If tree is small, you can transplant it to the new level.*

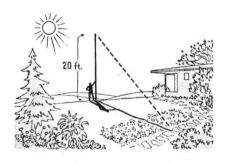

Before placing *a new tree, test shade patterns with a long pole to see how it will shade the house and garden.*

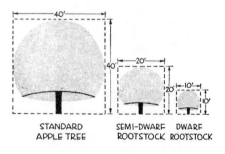

You can have *fruit trees in even the smallest garden if you choose one of the many excellent semi-dwarf or dwarf types.*

Large shade trees (40 to 80 feet) . . .

MORAINE LOCUST	NORWAY MAPLE	SILVER MAPLE	HOLLY OAK	COAST LIVE OAK	GINKGO	CHINESE ELM
Deciduous	Deciduous	Deciduous	Evergreen	Evergreen	Deciduous	Deciduous
Fast	Fast	Fast	Moderate	Moderate	Slow	Very fast

Medium shade trees (20 to 50 feet) . . .

APPLE	LITTLELEAF LINDEN	MODESTO ASH	SILK TREE	EASTERN REDBUD	WHITE MULBERRY
Deciduous	Deciduous	Deciduous	Deciduous	Deciduous	Deciduous
Slow	Moderate	Moderate	Moderate	Moderate	Slow

Small trees (15 to 30 feet) . . .

GOLDENRAIN	GLOSSY PRIVET	FLOWERING CRAB	FLOWERING CHERRY	HAWTHORN	RED HORSE CHESTNUT
Deciduous	Evergreen	Deciduous	Deciduous	Deciduous	Deciduous
Slow	Fast	Moderate to fast	Moderate to fast	Slow to moderate	Slow to moderate

Trees for screens (often topped at 20 to 30 feet) . . .

PITTOSPORUM	SILVER DOLLAR GUM	BUCKTHORN	INCENSE CEDAR	LIQUIDAMBAR	WHITE BIRCH
Evergreen	Evergreen	Evergreen	Evergreen	Deciduous	Deciduous
Most kinds fast	Moderate	Moderate	Moderate	Moderate	Moderate to fast

PERENNIALS

Perennials are long-time favorites of gardeners everywhere. Unlike annuals (see page 102), they continue to flower year after year, going into dormancy in winter after storing food in their roots for new growth the following spring.

As a group, perennials are a hardy lot, even in the coldest climates. Mild-climate gardeners enjoy an added plus-factor: Many perennials hold their leaves the year around.

Most perennials flower in summer, but some begin blooming in spring; the time of bloom depends largely on the region and climate. Chrysanthemums bloom in late summer and fall.

Although the great majority of perennials prefer a sunny location, some like shade.

MORE POPULAR THAN EVER

For many years, perennials were valued chiefly for their effectiveness in border

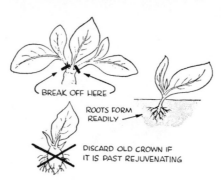

BREAK OFF HERE

ROOTS FORM READILY

DISCARD OLD CROWN IF IT IS PAST REJUVENATING

Bergenia increases easily. This large-leafed plant loves shade, produces clusters of flowers on stalks.

planting (still one of their best uses). Nowadays, however, the perennial picture is beginning to change as new ways of displaying them have brought out their long-overlooked versatility. The combinations that formed the classic perennial border have lost ground to simpler plantings. Now you see perennials used in much the same way as annuals: in massed beds, in edgings, as bulb covers and ground covers. Del-

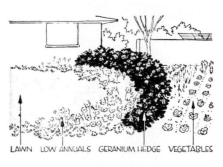

LAWN   LOW ANNUALS   GERANIUM HEDGE   VEGETABLES

Geraniums or pelargoniums make a sturdy, impressive, fast-growing hedge to divide separate garden areas.

phiniums are now planted in greater quantity than their annual equivalent, larkspur.

But, we're not trying to play one against the other. If lots of color is your dish, you need annuals *and* perennials. Seed companies and bedding plant growers make it easy for you to have plenty of both.

Try planting perennials as a ground

ACHILLEA (yarrow)
Sun. 8"-5'. Yellow, white. *A. Taggetea* good choice.

AGATHEA (felicia)
Sun, light shade. 18". Long bloom, good in border.

ALYSSUM, PERENNIAL
Sun. 4-12". Tiny bright golden-yellow flowers.

ASTER FRIKARTII
Sun. 18". Lavender-blue. Summer-fall. Very useful.

ASTILBE
Part shade. 2-3'. White, pink, rose, or red spikes.

CAMPANULA
Part shade. 6"-6'. Blue, white bells. Versatile.

CHRYSANTHEMUM
Sun. 1-3'. All colors but blue. Many flower forms.

COLUMBINE
Part shade. 2-4'. Rainbow hues. Spring-summer.

COREOPSIS
Sun. 3'. Yellow. Good with delphinium, Shasta daisy.

DAYLILY
Sun, part shade. 1-6'. Warm colors. Spring-fall.

DELPHINIUM
Sun. 1-6'. Unequalled blues; white, pink.

DIANTHUS
Sun. 6"-2'. Many colors, no blue. Very useful.

ENGLISH DAISY
Sun. 3-6". Many 2" flowers, tipped with pink or red.

GAILLARDIA
Sun. 1-2'. Warm colors. Excellent cut flower.

GAZANIA
Sun. 1'. Warm colors. Tough; good ground cover.

GERBERA (Transvaal daisy)
Sun. 18". Beautiful colors, no blue. Good cut flower.

HEUCHERA (coral bells)
Sun, part shade. 1-1½'. Coral, pink, white.

HOSTA
Shade. 2'. Glossy ribbed leaves. White, lilac.

HUNNEMANNIA
Sun. 2'. Flowers are yellow poppies. Mixes well.

JAPANESE ANEMONE
Shade or semi-shade. 2-4'. White, pink, rose.

MICHAELMAS DAISY
Sun. 1-5'. White, pink, red, lavender, purple.

PEONY, HERBACEOUS
Sun. 3-4'. Single, double flowers, white, pink, red.

PELARGONIUM (geranium)
Sun, light shade. 3'. Flowers white, many other colors.

PENSTEMON
Sun. 2-3'. All colors but yellow, orange. Cutting.

PHLOX (PERENNIAL)
Sun, part shade. 6"-5'. Many colors. Borders.

PHYSOSTEGIA
Sun. 3'. White, lavender, rose. Border, cut flower.

PRIMROSE
Part shade. 6"-3'. Many colors, types, sizes.

SEDUM SPECTABILE
Sun, part shade. 15-20" Gray leaves, pink flowers.

SHASTA DAISY
Sun. 1-3'. White, yellow centers. Superb cutting.

THALICTRUM
Part shade. 3-4'. Lavender, yellow. Use with lilies.

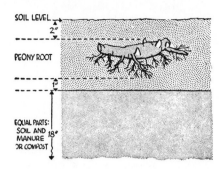

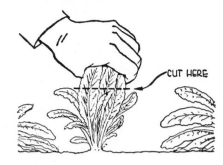

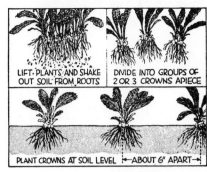

Peonies *feed heavily. Plant roots this way and you won't have to dig and divide for at least another 20 years.*

Polyantha primroses *will repeat bloom in fall if you cut them back after spring bloom and give them a feeding.*

Primrose *clumps need dividing every 2 years, after bloom season. Primroses like most soils, but rich loam is ideal.*

cover in narrow beds next to hedges, along driveways, as fillers among newly planted shrubs. If you are a container garden enthusiast, you'll find geraniums and chrysanthemums to be just two of many excellent pot subjects for gracing a patio, deck, or terrace.

If you plant them in a border, choose them carefully so they will work together in a harmonious pattern of color, form, size, and texture. Don't make the mistake of choosing plants which all bloom at the same time. A carefully planned border will have two crescendos of special glory—early summer and early autumn, but there should also be some color at other times (many gardeners include a few bulbs and annuals in the border).

Most perennials need dividing every several years (see techniques on page 14). Fall is a favorite time for dividing and replanting as well as for planting newly purchased perennials. Planting from flats is described on page 28; if you are planting from cans, see page 34. Get them in while ground is still warm, so roots can get a good start before winter.

Like most garden plants, perennials like rich soil, ample water, and good drainage.

Chrysanthemums: *For color in late summer and fall . . .*

The chrysanthemum is probably the best plant a new gardener can start with. Actually, it is not only one of the easiest but also one of the most rewarding perennials he can grow. The variety of flower forms, colors, and growth habits to choose from is truly amazing.

Flowers range from tiny pompom types about the size of a button all the way up to the large exhibition types that American women like to adorn themselves with at football games. Some look like daisies, some like anemones. There are types with long curling petals, either straight or with fish-hook tips that give them a spider-like appearance.

Plants of all sizes are available, tall growing, intermediate, and small—and you'll find a wide range of flower sizes as well as colors in each group.

Few plants adapt themselves as well to pot culture (see the plant rotation idea in the sketches to the right). During fall, when many garden plants are through flowering, potted chrysanthemums can be brought into play on a deck or patio to bring a splash of warm colors right outside the house where you can enjoy them. Even if you grow your mums in an out-of-the-way garden corner, you'll be able to cut armfuls of blooms for indoor arrangements. (Chrysanthemums are exceptional not only for their beauty as cut flowers but because they last for many days after cutting.)

Many gardeners like to cascade chrysanthemums from raised beds or hanging baskets. This is done by training types with pliable stems along a sturdy wire "stake," bent outward to a 45° angle. When the plant is a foot high, pinch out the tip to encourage side growth (this, incidentally, is a good idea for *all* chrysanthemums as well as many other perennials.) Pinch side shoots and make ties as the plant grows along the wire. Point wires south for best results, and keep bending them downward from time to time until the fully budded plant is finally hanging downward.

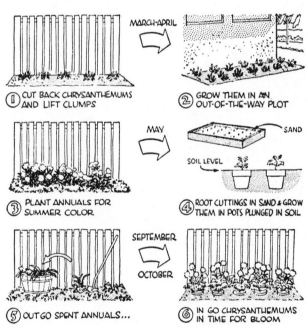

Chrysanthemum beds *can do double duty: Grow chrysanthemums in pots, and grow summer annuals in their place until fall.*

Chrysanthemums may be planted almost any time, but spring is generally best. You can also propagate them easily from softwood cuttings taken from young plants (see page 17).

Give chrysanthemums a sunny location, keep them well watered, and fertilize them once or twice during the growing season if your soil is on the poor side. Cut them to 8 inches from the ground after the last blossoms have faded.

ANNUALS

Annuals are fast-growing, temporary plants that bring color to your garden. Although they flower for one season only and then die, beginners and advanced gardeners alike enjoy them, not only because they are useful and rewarding but also because they are fun to grow.

HOW TO SOW

Starting annuals from seed is an experience no gardener should miss. You can sow seed directly in the ground (page 12) or in flats or other containers (page 13). You can also buy young plants at nurseries, by the dozen, in flats, or in individual containers. See page 28 for step-by-step instructions on setting out young plants.

Most annuals are summer flowering, but there are notable exceptions. On the facing page, where we show just a few of the many choices available, the following are all cool-season performers: calendula, dianthus, Iceland poppy, pansy and viola, stock, and some varieties of sweet pea.

Newcomers to seed gardening might start with marigold, nasturtium, and zinnia; all three are exceptionally easy and fast, and seeds are large enough to handle easily. Alyssum is the simplest to grow of the small-seeded kinds.

MANY VARIETIES, USES

Not only are there many kinds of annuals, but many varieties. Hybridizers are constantly coming up with newer and better strains. The time is long past, for example, when a zinnia was simply a zinnia; now there are big ones and small ones, flowers of many different forms and colors. The same holds true for just about any annual you can name.

As more and more varieties have come

along, the landscape use of annuals has continued to broaden. They bring flower color to your garden in any number of ways: mass plantings, in borders large or small, in front of fences or next to the house, as ground covers or vines, and in containers.

One of their best uses is as problem solvers. Used as fillers, they relieve the sparse appearance between newly planted shrubs, add color to bare bulb beds, and fill corners or gaps wherever you need them.

CUTTING

Many annuals are outstanding for cutting: aster, gypsophila, snapdragon, zinnia, stock, and sweet pea to name just a few. (The latter two are not only beautiful but fragrant.) Frequent cutting, and removal of dead blooms, also help to lengthen the bloom season.

PREPARE SOIL

Because most annuals are very fast growers (some take only 6 to 10 weeks from seed to flower) it is advisable to plant them in cultivated, reasonably rich soil so the young plants can put out their roots easily. A feeding or two, while plants are growing, also helps. Water them enough to keep the roots from drying out, but don't "drown" them.

When annuals are through blooming, pull them out by the roots and throw them away. Exceptions to this are snapdragons, which should be cut back to a foot or so from the ground when blooms fade, so they will come on for another flowering season. In mild climate, snapdragons left in the ground over winter will come back strong the following year. (Snapdragons, like pansies, violas, most hollyhocks, and certain other plants are actually *biennials* — slower growing plants with some of the characteristics of perennials. Actually, their culture is practically identical to that of annuals.)

Annuals *do best in well prepared soil.*

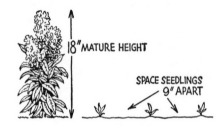

Spacing tip: *half of the mature height.*

This treatment *saves headaches later on.*

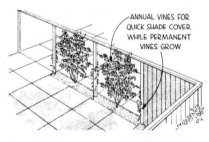

Annual vines *are good problem-solvers.*

Alyssum *gives a quick, colorful carpet.*

Nasturtiums *are favorites with children.*

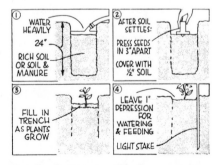

Trench planting: *try this for sweet peas.*

AFRICAN DAISY
Sun. 6-12". White, yellow, salmon. Flowers during day.

AGERATUM
Sun. 4-18". Lavender-blue. Low types good edgers.

ALYSSUM
Sun, part shade. 4-10". White, other colors. Good edger.

ASTER
Sun. 1-3'. Many colors. Often subject to wilt.

CALENDULA
Sun. 24". Yellow, cream, apricot. Cut them in bud.

CANDYTUFT
Sun. 6-15". White, pastels. Bulb cover (small types).

CELOSIA
Sun. 1-3'. Silky plumes in red, yellow, orange.

CLARKIA
Sun, light shade. 1-1½'. White, pink, red. Doubles, singles.

CLEOME
Sun, light shade. 4'. Pink, white flowers. Adaptable.

COSMOS
Sun. 2½-6'. Pink, orange, yellow, white flowers.

DAHLIA
(Unwin dwarf hybrids.) Sun. 1½-2'. Many colors.

DIANTHUS (pinks)
Sun. 12-16". Pink, rose, red, white. Borders, bouquets.

DIMORPHOTHECA
Sun. 6-12". White, yellow, orange. Gay free-flowering.

GYPSOPHILA
Sun. 1½-2'. Mass of white flowers. Filler in borders.

HOLLYHOCK
Sun. 5'. Many colors (no blue). Biennial; also annual type.

ICELAND POPPY
Sun. 18". White, orange, yellow, pink, scarlet. Many strains.

IMPATIENS
Part shade. 2'. White, pink. Light, graceful in effect.

LARKSPUR
Sun. 3-4'. Pastels, deeper shades. Use in backgrounds.

LOBELIA
Sun, half shade. 4-12". Blues, white. Good edger, trailer.

MARIGOLD
Sun. ½-3'. Yellow, orange shades. Many kinds available.

MORNING GLORY
(Vine.) Sun. Blue, white, red, pink. Blooms all summer.

NASTURTIUM
Sun, part shade. 1-6'. Most colors but blue. Trailing or bushy.

NICOTIANA
Partial shade. 1½-5'. White, pink, red. Fragrant at night.

PETUNIA
Sun, light shade. 6-24". Many colors. Good in borders.

PHLOX
Sun, light shade. 1-1½'. Many colors. Good mass effect.

PORTULACA
Sun. 6". Brilliant colors. Good for rock gardens, banks.

SCABIOSA
Sun. 3'. Many colors, no yellow. Combine with ageratum.

SCARLET SAGE
Sun. 1-3'. Fiery red. Effective; avoid color clash.

SHIRLEY POPPY
Sun. 2-3'. White, pink, red blooms like crepe paper.

SNAPDRAGON
Sun. 1½-4'. Many colors. Good in beds or as accents.

STOCK
Sun. 1½-3'. Beautiful colors (no real blue or yellow).

SWEET PEA
(Vine.) Sun; protect from wind. Some bloom into summer

TORENIA
Shade. 6". Lavender, purple, yellow. Good with ferns.

VERBENA
Sun. 8-10". Pastel, brilliant colors. Good ground cover, edger.

VIOLA (pansy)
Semi-shade. 6-12". Violas solid colors; pansies variegated.

ZINNIA
Full sun. ½-3'. Myriad colors, forms. Likes hot summers.

BULBS

An old expression, often heard in gardening circles, is: "The surest package of beauty you can buy is a healthy bulb."

It's true, and small wonder. A perfect flower is already formed within its sleek brown jacket. It seems fantastically simple that all you have to do to bring that flower out of hiding is to give the bulb a cool dark berth in the soil of your garden. For this small service, you reap a wonderful reward as the bulb continues to produce seasonal bloom year after year.

MANY KINDS

It is a common misconception to think of bulbs exclusively in connection with fall planting and spring flowers. Not that the spring-flowering kinds aren't magnificent—there's no more beautiful sight than a late winter or early spring garden bursting from gray dormancy into cheerful bulb color.

Actually, however, the term "bulbs" embraces several kinds of plants (see page 107), many of which bloom in summer or fall. While September marks the start of the season for planting spring bulbs, March is the month when you should begin to plant the summer and fall types.

Some of the most popular bulbs are listed in the chart beginning on page 106, with pertinent planting data. In the planting chapter, on page 33, we show techniques for open-ground planting of most kinds of bulbs (some, notably tuberous begonia and rhizomatic

When you set out bulbs this fall, mark the spots with small stakes; then set out the transplants...

Annuals *in bare bulb beds shouldn't be planted directly over bulbs. Use this procedure; or wait until bulb growth is above ground before you plant them.*

iris, cannot be planted this way; see the sketches in this chapter).

DON'T CUT FOLIAGE

When a bulb sends up foliage and flowers, the strength of the bulb itself is depleted. A gradual "recharging" period follows, during which the foliage transmits its energy back down to the bulb. It is highly important, therefore, not to cut the foliage until it has withered and yellowed.

If you dig the bulbs while foliage is still green, they must be cured by heeling them in or replanting them in some out-of-the-way place. A good way to hide the dying foliage without moving the bulbs is to make ties in it and fill in with some annuals (see page 39).

Daffodils and many other bulbs may be left in the ground for years until it's time to divide them. (In mild-winter regions, tulips will rot if not dug.) Tuberous begonias, dahlias, and gladiolus should always be dug and stored.

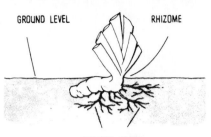

GROUND LEVEL   RHIZOME

SPREADER ROOTS

Bearded iris *and other rhizomes should be planted with top just beneath soil surface. If the rhizome has roots, spread them out carefully, cover with fine soil.*

For insurance, dust bulbs with an insecticide-fungicide before storing them.

LANDSCAPE USES

Bulbs inject surprise, excitement, and exhilaration into a garden which is otherwise quietly relaxing in shades of green and brown. Their clear colors and strong form can accentuate points of design—curves, angles, straight lines.

A mass planting of nodding yellow daffodils or tall, aristocratic tulips can be an impressive sight. Some home gardens have the space for this kind of bulb display, but others do not.

Happily, it isn't necessary to plant bulbs by the hundreds in order to use them effectively. A few dozen, or even a few handfuls, placed here and there where you can see and enjoy them, can be surprisingly effective.

Don't make the mistake of spreading them out too far. Plant them among your garden beds in little colonies where their colorful flowers will catch

---

Tuberous begonias: *Summer-blooming beauties...*

Tuberous begonias are show-offs. So they won't upstage other flowers, it is best to plant them all by themselves or combine them with a neutral background planting.

There are several types. Doubles have the largest blooms (up to 8 inches in diameter). When planting, remember that blooms will point in same direction as leaves.

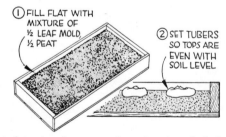

① FILL FLAT WITH MIXTURE OF ½ LEAF MOLD, ½ PEAT

② SET TUBERS SO TOPS ARE EVEN WITH SOIL LEVEL

Start tubers *indoors in winter or early spring, 6 weeks before you plan to set them out. Rooting medium should be moist. Keep them at 65°-75° in good light (no sun).*

BUD

IN EARLY SPRING, COOL AIR-HIGHER HUMIDITY ENABLES YOUNG PLANTS TO TOLERATE MORE SUN

IF YOU CAN GET THEM THIS FAR—THE BATTLE'S WON, THEN.....

MOVE THEM INTO SHADE

You can *set up your own weather control if you grow begonias in pots. Plunge pots in ground with an eastern exposure in early spring, move them to filtered shade later.*

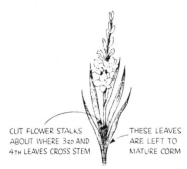

Gladiolus *corms get next year's energy from foliage; don't cut foliage until it turns brown and it's time to dig (this is true with most bulbs).*

CUT FLOWER STALKS ABOUT WHERE 3RD AND 4TH LEAVES CROSS STEM

THESE LEAVES ARE LEFT TO MATURE CORM

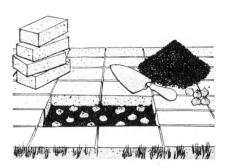

Set bulbs *in place of bricks in patio. Follow up with pansies, lobelia, or alyssum; or remove bulbs, cure them in a trench, and replace bricks.*

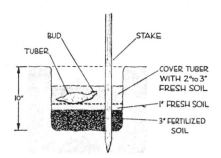

Dahlia *tubers should be planted like this in spring. Gradually fill in hole as sprouts appear. Stakes are particularly important if you are growing tall varieties.*

BUD   STAKE
TUBER
COVER TUBER WITH 2" to 3" FRESH SOIL
1" FRESH SOIL
3" FERTILIZED SOIL
10"

the eye. When you use bulbs like this, try for a natural effect rather than spacing them formally. Some gardeners throw a handful or two on the ground in the vicinity where they want them, and plant them exactly where they fall.

The possibilities for brightening odd corners are limitless. Try an informal planting of crocus at the base of a flowering tree. Or, for a formal touch, plant a carefully spaced border of hyacinths around a planting pocket to frame the base of a vine or some other favorite plant.

Bulbs are excellent container subjects. Daffodils, tulips, lilies, and cyclamen are only a few of many examples.

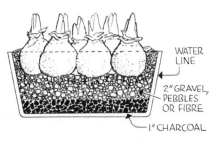

WATER LINE
2" GRAVEL, PEBBLES OR FIBRE
1" CHARCOAL

Some bulbs *(daffodil, hyacinth) can be forced in a bowl, brought indoors for Christmas. Plant as shown, keep in cool dark place 6 weeks, then bring them into a light room. When growth reaches 5 inches, move to a sunny south window; they'll bloom in 3 weeks. Forcing weakens bulbs; don't force same ones next year.*

CHARTING BULB BEDS
WEATHERPROOF LABELS ON STAKES DEFINE ROWS -KEEP BULB NAMES STRAIGHT

"What's planted where" *can be a bulb gardener's dilemma. It pays to make a planting chart at the time you put them in, and keep it in a handy place for future reference. If you plan to dig them up after bloom, mark the rows where you planted them with stakes labeled with names and varieties.*

How to grow bulbs in pots . . .

Using daffodils as models, here we show the two most important steps in potting bulbs.

To protect against soil insects and rot, treat the bulb with a fungicide-insecticide dust before planting—a wise precaution with bulbs planted either in pots or in the ground.

For mass bloom in pots, place bulbs so they almost touch. When leaves are 3 or 4 inches high, feed with complete liquid fertilizer; repeat every 2 weeks until flower buds show color. Keep soil evenly moist.

After bloom, keep watering until the leaves start turning yellow. When foliage is completely dry, tip bulbs out of pots, and remove dried-up foliage and any soil still adhering to bulbs.

In autumn, re-pot in fresh soil mix, or plant in the ground. You can grow the same bulbs in pots for 2 years.

Six daffodils *(double-nose) in a 9-inch pot. Procedure: Cover drainage hole with pieces of broken pot. Add soil mix (equal parts loam, sand, peat moss) plus tablespoon of bone meal. Insert bulbs; cover them with soil mix so that the tops are just at soil level; water.*

DARROW M. WATT

Place potted bulbs *in a level trench. Cover with 6 inches of wood shavings, sawdust, peat moss, or ground bark. Keep the covering and soil in pots evenly moist. When bulbs have strong roots and foliage appears, lift pots and put them in a warm spot where they have ample sunlight.*

Two dozen bulb favorites . . .

	NAME	KIND, HARDINESS	FLOWER COLORS	PLANTING TIME	PLANTING DEPTH	SPACING; LOCATION	BLOOM SEASON
	ACHIMINES	Rhizome (tender)	Red, pink, blue, white, purple, violet	Jan.-April	½ to 1"	1". Part shade	Summer
	ACIDANTHERA	Corm (tender)	Creamy white	Spring	3-4"	4-6". Sun	Summer
	AGAPANTHUS	Tuberous rootstock (half-hardy)	Blue, white	Evergreen: spring or fall. Deciduous: fall	Up to root crown	2-3". Sun, part shade	Summer
	ANEMONE (Windflower)	Tuberous rootstock (hardy, half-hardy)	Blue, red, pink, white	Fall	1"	6". Sun, light shade.	Spring
	CANNA	Tuberous rootstock (half-hardy)	Many (no blue)	May, June	5"	10-18". Sun	Summer
	CROCUS	Corm (hardy)	Yellow, orange, lavender, purple, white	Fall	2-3"	2-4". Sun, light shade.	Fall to spring; depends on species
	CYCLAMEN	Tubers, corms	pink, white Crimson, rose,	June-August	Hardy; ½"; florists' type: tuber half above soil	6-10". Filtered sun.	Fall to spring; depends on species
	DAHLIA	Tuberous rootstock (tender)	Many (no blue)	Spring	See page 105	3-4'. Sun.	Late summer, fall
	GALANTHUS (Snowdrop)	True bulb (hardy)	White	Fall	3-4"	2-3". Sun, part shade	Spring
	GLADIOLUS	Corm (tender to half-hardy)	Many colors and shades	Spring (winter in desert regions)	4"	4". Sun	Summer
	HYACINTH	True bulb (hardy)	Red, pink, blue, purple, white	Sept.-Nov.	4-6"	6-8". Sun, light shade	Spring
	IRIS	Rhizome or bulb (many species hardy)	Many colors	July-Oct.	Bulbs: 4". Rhizomes: (see page 104)	Bulbs: 3-4". Rhizomes: 1'. Sun	Spring. Some species repeat bloom
	LILY	True bulb (hardy)	Many colors	Fall	(See chart on page 33)	6-12". Sun or part shade.	Summer
	LYCORIS (Spider lily)	True bulb (tender or half-hardy)	Yellow, pink, rose, red	Late summer or fall	3-6" (in pots, expose tops)	4-6". Part shade	Spring
	MUSCARI (Grape hyacinth)	True bulb (hardy)	Blue, white	Fall	2"	2-4". Sun, light shade	Spring
	NARCISSUS (Daffodil, others)	True bulb (hardy)	Yellow, orange, white, bicolors	Fall	3-6" (depends on size)	3-8". Sun, light shade.	Late winter, spring
	NERINE	True bulb (half hardy or tender)	Pink, rose, red	Aug.-Oct.	Upper half above soil in pot.	3 bulbs to a 6" pot. Sun	Late summer, early fall

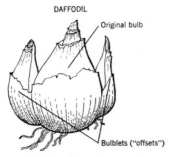	RANUNCULUS	Tuber (half-hardy)	Many colors (no blue)	Fall	2"	3-4". Sun	Spring
	SCHIZOSTYLIS	Rhizome (tender or half-hardy)	Rose-pink	Spring	Just under soil surface	6". Sun	Fall
	SINNINGIA SPECIOSA (Gloxinia)	Tuber (tender)	Blue, purple, pink, red, white	Dec.-March	1"	5" pot. Good light, no sun	Spring
	TUBEROUS BEGONIA	Tuber (tender)	Many colors (no blue)	Winter, early spring	(See page 104)	Grow in pots. Filtered sun	Summer to fall
	TULIP	True bulb (hardy)	Many colors	Fall	4-6" (depends on size)	4-8". Sun, light shade	Spring
	ZANTEDESCHIA (Calla lily)	Rhizome (tender to half-hardy)	White, gold, red, pink	Spring or fall	2-6" (depends on climate, variety)	1-2'. Sun or part shade.	Spring, summer
	ZEPHYRANTHES	True bulb (half-hardy)	Rose, pink, yellow, white	Spring (summer, fall in mild areas)	1-2"	3". Sun	Fall

What is a bulb, anyway?

The term "bulb" is one that is loosely applied to any plant that has a swollen or thickened basal portion. However, only about half of these plants are true bulbs. The rest are bulb-like and have their own special designations. All, nevertheless, have one thing in common: They are food storage bins that the plant can draw on to start active growth after the season of dormancy.

Ways to divide bulbs are explained on page 16.

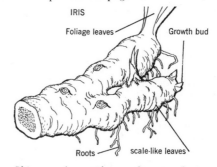

True bulb. *Short underground stem on solid basal plate, surrounded by fleshy leaves that store food for future growth. Outer scales are dry, papery. Bulblets grow larger each year until it's time to divide and replant them.*

Corm. *Swollen underground portion of stem, covered with one or more dead leaf bases. Food storage in solid tissue (not in scales). New corms form atop old corm; throw old shriveled one away, save the new ones to plant next year.*

Rhizome. *A creeping underground stem, often thick with stored food. Foliage leaves and flower stalk arise from buds on upper side, roots grow from below. Rhizomes can be cut into divisions (each must have at least one growth bud).*

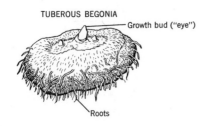

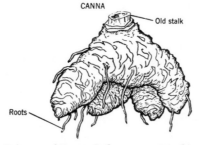

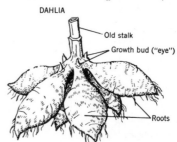

Tuber. *Short, fat, underground stem for food storage. Doesn't creep like rhizome. Usually knobby with growth buds called "eyes" (each is a scale-like leaf with buds in its axil). Large tubers are divided in much the same way as rhizomes.*

Tuberous rhizome *(tuberous rootstock). A slender underground stem (rhizome) that is thickened at the end into a tuber-like structure for storing food. If the rhizome is branched, it may have a tuber at the end of each branch.*

Tuberous roots. *These are actually roots (not stems) with thickened food storage structures. They can be divided in same way as rhizomes or tubers, if sections are cut so as to include the "eye" on the old stem base of the plant.*

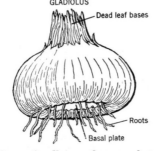

ROSES

The rose is easily the most popular of all flowers—and for good reason. The matchless beauty of the blooms is in itself enough to qualify this ancient shrub for top ranking. Add to this their fragrance, unending variety of forms and colors, long bloom season, and wide adaptability. Small wonder that roses are beloved by gardeners everywhere.

A rose garden, probably more than any other kind, reflects the talents and diligence of the gardener who maintains it. On the facing page is a year-round guide to rose care; if you follow it conscientiously, you will have plants of which you can be proud.

At the outset, buy good plants. Be sure those you select have 3 to 5 thick, healthy canes and roots that are not dried out. If you order plants by mail, buy only from a reputable nursery company.

TYPES AND VARIETIES

There are many kinds of roses, encompassing literally thousands of varieties. The types listed here are those most popular in the gardens of today. We have suggested a few time-proven varieties as a starting point for the beginner; it should be remembered, however, that many magnificent new introductions are being added to the list each year, and some will replace the current favorites.

Hybrid teas. These are the aristocrats of the rose world. Flowers are beautifully formed and generally large, and buds are long and graceful. Examples: Peace (yellow shaded cerise), Charlotte Armstrong (rose pink), Chrysler Imperial (red), First Love (pink).

Floribundas. Smaller-flowered and generally lower-growing than hybrid teas, this class is famed for its masses of bloom borne almost continuously from spring to fall. Examples: Circus (multicolor), Sarabande (scarlet-orange). Several good polyantha types, from which floribundas are descended, are still available. Examples: Margo Koster, The Fairy.

Grandifloras. Descended from crosses between floribundas and hybrid teas, this class combines many good features of both. Plants are vigorous, and usually tall growing. Examples: Queen Elizabeth (pink), Montezuma (burnt orange).

Climbers. Many of the best varieties are sports of hybrid teas, floribundas, and grandifloras. Example: Climbing Peace. Pillar types climb to only 10 or 12 feet, and are ideal for some situations. Example: High Noon (yellow).

Tree Roses. Many hybrid teas, floribundas, and grandifloras are budded on tall-caned understocks and sold as standards

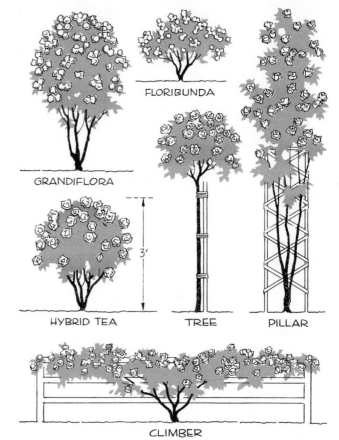

Here are *some of the best known classes and types of roses.*

24 or 40 inches tall. They are excellent for lining walkways or adding a tall accent wherever needed.

Trailers. These hardy climbers have pliable canes that hug the ground, making them good choices for ground covers. Example: Mermaid.

Bush types. Noted for their landscape value in row plantings more than beauty of individual blooms, some species roses and their hybrids make excellent "living fences." Examples: *Rosa multiflora, R. hugonis,* Red Robin.

Old Roses. It's getting harder to find the fragrant, enchanting favorites of yesteryear, but some are still obtainable by mail order. Examples: La Reine Victoria, Souvenir de Malmaison.

Miniatures. These tiny specimens are excellent for rock gardens and container planting. Buds the size of popcorn kernels open into perfect blooms less than an inch in diameter. Example: Eleanor.

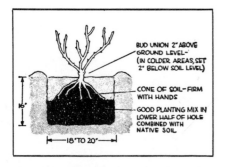

Plant roses *like this, or use "transition soil" method shown on page 32.*

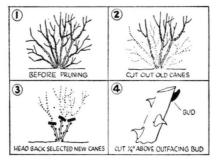

Low pruning, *popular in cold areas. See page 61 for more information.*

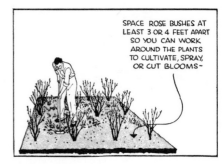

Closely planted *roses are hard to tend, won't have ample root room.*

Rose culture the year around . . .

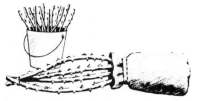

JANUARY

Buy or order bare-root roses. Plant bare root now if you live in a mild climate (see page 108). Otherwise, keep roots moist until planting time. A good mix: 7 parts soil, 1½ parts peat moss, 1 part manure. After planting, mound mulch around canes to prevent drying.

FEBRUARY

This is also a good planting month in most mild winter areas; it's also a good time to prune established roses. In cold regions, wait a month or so until leaf buds begin to swell before pruning. A dormant spray, at winter strength, is helpful at this time.

MARCH

A good planting month in some cold regions. In warm climates, fertilize; begin all-purpose spray program, but not while new leaves are still small and tender, or you'll burn them. Pull away mulch or soil covering canes; renew mulch to a depth of 2 inches.

APRIL

In cold regions, put in bare-root plants. This is also a good month for mild-climate gardeners to buy and plant roses in cans or tarpaper containers, following the procedure shown on page 34. Continue spraying established roses. Water if necessary.

MAY

Shop for plants in cans; many are in bloom now, and you'll have a chance to see what flowers look like. Spray or dust regularly, keeping a special lookout for mildew. In hot, dry regions, soak plants deeply every 2 weeks if soil is heavy, oftener if soil is light.

JUNE

This is a wonderful month for cutting flowers and enjoying the rose garden in its first flush of full bloom. Always cut above 5 strong, healthy leaves and above an outside-facing bud. Spray and water. Feed immediately after peak bloom to encourage new growth.

JULY

Spray, water. Remove suckers (growth that sometimes grows from below the graft union). July needn't be a "summer doldrums" month for roses—if your garden contains several modern varieties, chances are that some of them will be blooming in July.

AUGUST

Cut faded blooms and twiggy wood. Pinch back tip growth on new basal canes when 12 to 18 inches high to encourage side branching. Renew mulch. In cold-winter areas, give a final feeding to encourage late summer bloom. Spray and water.

SEPTEMBER

In mild climates, a final feeding now will encourage fall bloom; also, continue to spray and water (in cold climates, you'll be tapering off the latter two about now). Rose nurseries mail catalogs this month; order new varieties that may be in short supply.

OCTOBER

This is an excellent bloom month in mild winter regions, although some varieties—particularly many of the older ones — are through flowering. Keep faded blooms cut. Dig out plants that haven't performed well and make room for new varieties.

NOVEMBER

Some roses are still blooming in mild climates. In cold areas, protect plants by mounding soil well above bud union. In *extremely* cold regions, lay tree roses and climbers on their side, cover with soil and straw (see the *Sunset* book, *How to Grow Roses*).

DECEMBER

Stop watering established plants to encourage them to go dormant. Knock down water basins around plants so winter rains will drain away instead of "drowning" your roses. This is a good month to browse through catalogs and order new varieties for next season.

LAWN GRASSES

There are more than 40 kinds of grasses for home gardens, all of which come under one of two broad classifications: *cool-season* or *subtropical*. If you live in a region where winter brings heavy frosts or snow, you'll have to grow the hardy cool-season types. In mild-winter regions, subtropicals thrive with far less care than cool-season types and therefore merit your consideration. (You can grow cool-season grasses in southern regions, but it's a constant fight to keep the ever-present subtropicals from taking over.)

COOL-SEASON GRASSES

Comprising this group are the bents, fine fescues, coarse fescues, blue grasses, rye grasses, redtop, and clover. You can buy them straight or in mixes.

Bents. High-maintenance; require careful attention to mowing, fertilizing, watering, disease control. Erect and creeping types are available; erect types should be mowed to ¾ inch to 1 inch, creeping types to ½ inch. Don't give bents too much shade.

Fine fescues. Found in most fine-leafed lawn mixes. The rolled leaves look like tiny soft needles. Easily grown in most soils; fairly drought-resistant. Cut at 1½ to 2 inches. Shade tolerant.

Blue grasses. Widely grown. Available in many mixes. Most types do best if mowed to 1½ inches. Only one type, Poa Trivialis, does well in shade—and it does *exceptionally* well.

Rye grasses. Perennial and annual types available. Both are fast growers but have bunchy growth habit. Often hard to mow. Keep at 1½ inches.

Coarse fescues. Rugged; good for athletic fields, children's play yards. Mow to 2 inches. Best in full sun.

Clover. Popular in some low-maintenance grass mixes. Attracts bees, stains clothing badly. Rapid grower. Under good conditions it manufactures its own nitrogen, minimizing need for lawn feeding. Mow to about 2 inches.

Redtop. Has few good points; often included in mixtures as a temporary "nurse" grass.

SUBTROPICAL GRASSES

Zoysia grasses. Very slow to establish, but eventually make a strong, dense turf (no weeds, Burmuda, insects, or diseases). Dormant in winter. Quite drought-resistant, easy to maintain. Mowing height ½ to 1½ inches, depending on variety. Sun or shade.

Bermuda grasses. Fine-textured. Recent hybrid strains are very popular. Winter green is assisted by early fall fertilization and removal of thatch. Mow to ½ inch. Won't take shade.

St. Augustine grass. A coarse, wide-bladed, dark green grass, extremely easy to maintain. Has short dormancy. You need a power mower for this one; cut at 1½ inches. Takes some shade.

KEEPING CUT FLOWERS FRESH

Keeping quality of a cut flower is influenced by: (1) maturity of the flower and time of day when it is cut; (2) temperature at which the bloom is kept after it is removed from the plant; (3) amount of water that can be kept in the stem and flower after cutting; and (4) rate of respiration.

Cutting flowers. Maturity of the flower is a very important factor. Flowers picked too green fail to open; those past their prime have begun to deteriorate. There is no general rule regarding the stage of development at which flowers will keep longest if cut; experience with each kind will be your best guide.

For many years experts advocated cutting flowers in the early morning when they were fresh and full of water. But recent studies show that some flowers, particularly roses, in late afternoon have a high sugar content that prolongs the life of the cut flower.

Temperature. It is always best to keep cut flowers in the coolest spot possible. It is a good idea to store them in a cool, dark corner of a garage or basement the first few hours after cutting. When they are arranged, keep the vases away from furnace outlets or direct sunlight.

Keeping cut stems turgid. To keep stems full of water, it is necessary to keep the water-conducting tubes open and cleared of bacteria. To accomplish this, recut stems under water, or immediately before putting them in water; use a sharp knife or shears, making a slanting cut. Be sure the container in which you arrange the flowers is clean; remove any leaves below the water line. (Submerged foliage decays quickly.)

Use warm water in the container in which you place flowers immediately after cutting them. Let them stand until the water cools to room temperature (about two hours). Warm water moves more quickly through the stem than does cold.

Preservatives. Flower preservatives, added to the water, retard deterioration of the plant cells. The commercial flower preservatives contain food for the cut bloom in the form of sugar, an acidifier to prevent bacterial growth, and a mild fungicide to kill any fungi that may be present in the water.

For best results add it to the water in which the freshly cut flowers are placed, as well as to the water in the container in which the flowers are arranged.

1. Use a sharp knife or shears to cut flowers. Make slanting cut so stems don't rest flush with bottom and block water intake. Remove leaves covered by water in container

2. Place freshly cut stems in deep container of warm water (about 110°). Let it cool to room temperature before making up flower arrangements

3. If flowers are slightly wilted, cover heads with a sheet of polyethylene film, a paper sack, or newspaper to reduce transpiration, regain turgidity

4. Add a preservative to the water to kill fungus and bacteria, provide food for cut blooms, and eliminate need for changing water daily

5. To keep cut flowers fresh longer, place your arrangement in a cool spot away from direct sunlight

Garden Specialties

ROBERT COX

VEGETABLES

From all over the world, and from among thousands of vastly different plants, nature has given us a little more than three dozen edible pods, leaves, fruits, and roots that are our popular vegetables. Man has grown them for centuries, with many improved varieties adding to the enjoyment and the reward; but a beet is still a beet and a shallot is still a shallot.

There's no need for a king-sized plot —they are a thing of the past, except in rural communities where space is plentiful. You can grow a surprising number of vegetables in a space only 10 by 10 feet. Some have enough ornamental value to combine well with your regular garden plantings.

The all-important, no-exceptions fundamental of growing good vegetables: A vegetable is a full-draft plant needing all the moisture, nutrients, and sunlight it can get. If you skimp on these needs, you check its growth, and it can never fully recover.

Most vegetables are easily started from seed (see pages 12 and 13). Many kinds are sold in flats; transplant them much as you would annuals (page 28).

Cultivate soil where you're going to plant vegetables, working in a complete commercial fertilizer or some well-rotted manure. Once plants are growing, pull weeds as you see them so they won't compete for nutrients.

Caution. When you spray or dust vegetables with an insecticide or fungicide, *follow label directions to the letter,* both as to strength and timing. Don't spray ripening vegetables if you can avoid it—many chemicals have a residual toxicity that will make the vegetables unsafe to eat for days or even weeks.

The edible leaves

Under this heading are two very easy-to-grow and desirable home garden plants (Swiss chard and leaf lettuce), and two others so challenging that few find the growing worthwhile. Spinach and celery are in the challenging class (99 out of 100 gardeners would rather buy them at the store).

Spinach

Sow spinach in July to September so it can grow to maturity during fall, winter, and spring. Long daylight of late spring and summer heat make it go to seed too fast. It requires a rich soil that drains well. After seedlings start growing, thin plants to 4 inches apart.

Swiss chard

Ideal for any garden (even as your only vegetable crop), easy to grow, pretty, it yields continually through the first summer without bolting to seed. Grow it in any sunny planting position—among flowers or whatever. Young seedlings transplant easily. Space each plant at least 12 inches from any other. Tasty rhubarb chard has red stems, attractive leaves, is valued for floral arranging.

Celery

Take this on if you're looking for a horticultural challenge. It doesn't tolerate very high or low temperatures, is a heavy user of water and nutrients, needs sandy or silty loam. Planted in early spring in most regions. Seeds are slow to germinate; start them indoors 2 months ahead of planting time.

All the lettuces

Illustrated at left are representative varieties of the four kinds of lettuce. From top to bottom: (1) crisphead or heading; (2) butterhead; (3) a kind known variously as leaf, bunching, loose leafed, or loosehead; and (4) romaine. Crisphead is trickiest to grow because ideal heading comes only with monthly mean temperatures between 55° and 60°. If it's too hot, central stalk elongates and loses quality. Other lettuces are easy to grow. Butterhead varieties are loosely folded with smooth yellow center leaves. Leaf lettuces are best for growing through hot season; cut leaves from outside the cluster as you need them. Plant rows of several different kinds at intervals through the year to keep a continuous, varied supply coming on. Space leafy varieties 5 to 10 inches apart in the row, heading types 10 to 18 inches apart.

The legumes

Peas and beans have an obvious botanical relationship, but little else in common. Peas are a cool weather crop; beans need heat. Plant beans in late spring to midsummer; plant peas in fall, winter, or early spring.

Peas

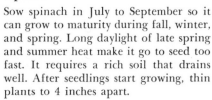

Plant in water-retentive but fast-draining soil. Place a little fertilizer beside the plants when they are 9 inches high. The edible pod or sugar peas, delicious and served in Chinese restaurants, are not widely sold in stores. Grow them yourself. (They do not do well in warm-winter areas.)

Beans

Beans may not sprout if soil is too cold or too dense. Plant when warm weather comes (April in many places). Condition heavy soil to make it soft. Pole beans, the kind you start twining up sticks or strings, mature 10 days to 2 weeks more slowly than bush beans, but yield more.

The edible roots

The root crops listed here are not as closely related as you might think. Carrot and parsnip belong in the parsley family. Radish and the turnip are mustards. Salsify is one of the daisies or composites. Beet belongs to the goosefoot family. Nevertheless, all have certain requirements in common: Sow as early in spring as possible; they grow when it's cool and, generally speaking, heat can reduce their quality. Old manure blended into soil before planting makes them grow well, as does a thin band of commercial fertilizer placed 2 inches out from the row. Seeds are often slow to germinate; give them continual moisture to make them sprout and then grow vigorously.

Carrots

Sow carrot seeds rather thickly (20 to 30 seeds per foot of row) because they germinate unevenly. Rocky or clay soil makes roots branch and grow crooked. Continual moisture and a non-crusted soil over the seed are much needed to bring carrots up. When tops are 2 inches high, thin them out to leave 1½ inches between each plant and, at the same time, apply a thin band of commercial fertilizer 2 inches out from the row.

Turnips and rutabagas

Even if you don't like turnips, they are pretty. Part of the fun is the choice of color and shape by variety. Colors: white, white topped with purple, creamy yellow. Shapes: globe, flattened globe. Rutabaga is a tasty kind of turnip with large, yellowish roots. In cold winter areas, plant turnips or rutabagas now for early summer harvest or in July or August for fall harvest. In mild winter areas, grow as a winter crop by planting September through March.

Beets

Plant a 10-foot row now in soil that won't crust, keep it moist, and in some 60 days it will yield 50 delicious, tender small beets (tenderest at 1½ to 2 inches in diameter). Meanwhile, when plants are 5 inches high, begin pulling out excess so that by the time the remaining plants are 60 days old (harvest time) they will be 4 inches apart. The thinnings (beets and tops) can be cooked as very good greens.

Parsnips

They are related to the carrot, with culture quite similar, but growth much slower—four months from seed to harvest. In cold winter areas, best idea is to sow seed in late spring, let them grow through summer, harvest in fall, and leave the excess in the ground to be dug as needed all winter. In milder climates, parsnips will rot if left in the ground; sow seed in fall and harvest in spring.

Radishes

You can pull radishes for the table three weeks after you sow the seed. Speedy growth and relatively easy culture make them popular. They need continual moisture and some added nutrients to grow well. Supply the nutrients by blending rotted manure into the soil before planting or—about 10 days after planting—apply a side dressing as for carrots, or feed with liquid fertilizer.

Salsify

It looks something like a parsnip and has a creamy white flesh that tastes a little like oysters. Culture is much the same as for parsnips: Plant in a rich, deep, sandy soil, spaded deep. It takes 150 days to grow to maturity. Cooked, mashed salsify, mixed with butter and beaten egg, can be made into patties and sautéed until brown to make mock oysters.

Beans: *Train up a single pole; or train several plants at once by adding wires.*

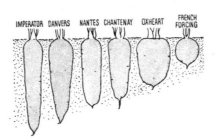

Carrots: *If your soil is heavy, grow a short, stubby variety such as Oxheart; or*

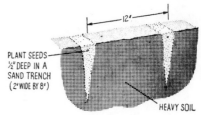

sow seed in a sand trench if you want to grow one of the longer varieties.

The vine crops

All these familiar summer crops, or their wild ancestors, came from the tropics. The vine crops simply cannot stand a frost. So their season is limited to the time between the last frost and the first. In regions where there are only about four months between frosts, vine crop growers have to start early, often planting the seeds in paper cups or boxes a few weeks before the last frost date and then setting out the little seedlings from the cups when it's safe. All vine crops take in nutrients voraciously. To grow them well, put a shovelful of manure in a hole under the spot where you will plant the seeds, cover with soil, and then plant seeds. Keep weeds out of the beds; water often.

Squashes and pumpkins

There are two basic types of squash. *Summer squash,* such as scallop or zucchini, takes only about two months to ripen from seed. *Winter squashes* have hard shells; they need three or four months to ripen, as do *pumpkins,* a close cousin to the squash family. Plant seeds in late spring, when weather is beginning to warm up. Give them plenty of water and lots of room. To avoid rot, make sure ripening fruit rests on dry ground.

Cucumbers

Owners of small gardens have difficulty giving needed room for any of the vine crops because they all range wide and need at least a 5 by 5-foot ground area. Cucumbers, by their light weight, adapt well to being trained up trellises, thereby saving much room. Plant them 18 inches apart, train the center stem vertically up the trellis to the top, then pinch the top off and train the side branches sideways. Otherwise, grow in the same manner as pumpkins, squash, and melons.

Melons

To ripen to full sweetness, a melon needs from $2\frac{1}{2}$ to 4 months of heat. Foggy summer days or cool days cannot be accepted. Grow melons according to the same full-draft scheme as the other vine crops; however, they can't develop the desired sweetness without the needed heat. Watermelons need more heat than other melons and more space than other vine crops (8 feet by 8 feet). Of all melons, cantaloups are easiest to grow because they ripen fastest.

The lone cereal

As you might expect from a vegetable in the same family as bamboo and lawn grass, sweet corn has some special ways that must be reckoned with if you are going to get a good crop. It must be planted after soil has warmed and frosts are past. It must be planted in a series of parallel rows so that wind can distribute pollen effectively—otherwise few or no kernels form in the ears. It needs all the

water it can get after growth starts, and especially at tasseling and after silking. It thrives on heat. After ears form, the kernels can go from the watery-kernel stage (immature) to the milky stage (just right) to the tough stage (too starchy to be good) in just a day. But if weather is cool at ripening time, this progression may take a week. You've probably heard this before: Picked corn changes sugar to starch very fast, faster than field-to-market shipment. There's nothing like the taste of sweet corn picked fresh and cooked immediately. Try it.

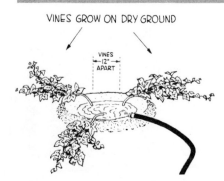

Squash, pumpkins: *Sow seeds in a circular irrigating dike about 2 feet across; let the vines spread out onto dry ground.*

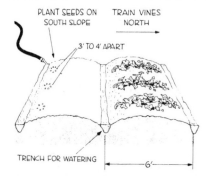

Melons: *Grow in gently rounded, raised beds, 6 feet from center to center (allow 8 feet for watermelons).*

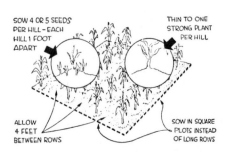

Corn: *Plant several parallel rows so wind can distribute pollen. Run rows north to south for maximum sun.*

The bulbs

A great convenience is being overlooked by too many new gardeners today—the bulb crops. It's easy to grow just a few of these plants in some garden pocket. The crops remain growing and available, like money in the bank, most of the year, waiting to be harvested.

All the onions

Onions are really easy to grow; they need only a fairly rich soil, and regular watering. Applications of fertilizer several times a year will make them grow well. Plant onion sets (baby onions from seed stores) all winter and up through April in mild climates; plant them in earliest spring in harsh-winter climates. After three weeks, you can begin to pull them as green onions—white, moist, perishable types. Or sow seed in early spring. Onions need about 5 months from seed, 3 or 4 months from sets, to grow to maturity. After tops die back, pull the onions out of the ground and let them cure on the surface for several days. The dry onions can be stored for considerable periods of time.

Garlic

Seed stores and some mail order seed houses sell mother bulbs for planting. They will look like garlic bulbs from the grocery, only firmer. Break them up into cloves and plant base downward, 1 to 2 inches deep and 2 to 3 inches apart, in rows 12 inches apart. One or two dozen cloves will be plenty. Culture is the same as for onions; harvest the same way as dry onions.

Leeks

An onion relative, leek doesn't form a bulb. Grow from seed. As the plants grow, draw earth up around the fat, round stems to make the bottoms white and mild.

Shallots

This mild, sweet onion goes in many gourmet recipes. Grow from sets like the dry onion. Plant in fall 6 to 8 inches apart. Fertilize once or twice during the growing season. Dig in spring. To blanch, ridge about 4 inches of soil up around the plants 5 weeks before harvest.

The perennials

These plants grow tall, last from year to year. Plant roots in late winter or early spring. Nurserymen often put roots in cans to be available all year.

Asparagus

Dig 12-inch trenches, work 6 inches of rotted manure into the bottoms, and water thoroughly. Plant asparagus crowns 2 weeks later. Set them 12 inches apart; spread roots. Crowns should be 6 inches below top of trench. Cover with 2 inches of soil; water well. As plants grow, fill trench but never cover tips. First year, let plants alone. Cut spears the second year.

Rhubarb

It's best in cooler sections, but you can grow it almost anywhere. Give it some shade in hot inland gardens. Plant at least 3 or 4 plants. Space roots 2 to 4 feet apart, setting bud top 4 inches deep. Water slowly and deeply. Let plants grow through two seasons before harvesting.

Artichokes

This gourmet's favorite likes cool weather, but can't take cold winters (it does best in the coastal belt of central California). Plant divisions in early spring, with base of new leafy shoots just above ground; you'll get full production in about 18 months.

CUT 1½" BELOW BASE OF BUD

Artichokes: *Cut when buds are about 2 to 4 inches in diameter, but before the bracts start to separate or open.*

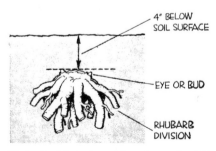
4" BELOW SOIL SURFACE
EYE OR BUD
RHUBARB DIVISION

Rhubarb: *Plant in spring (or early fall in mild climates). Before planting, enrich the soil with humus and fertilizer.*

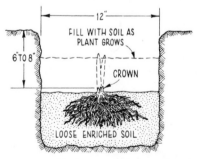
12"
FILL WITH SOIL AS PLANT GROWS
6 TO 8"
CROWN
LOOSE ENRICHED SOIL

Asparagus: *Plant crowns in trenches in early spring. Spread roots out evenly. You'll be adding the last soil by summer.*

The cole crops

This is the cabbage family, all members of which waft the same unmistakable fragrance through the house while being cooked. As vegetable crops, their two worst enemies are hot days, which make them go to seed, and aphids. Cool coastal areas don't get enough summer heat to faze these crops. But in other areas, plant in August, September, or October so the plants (90 to 150 days to maturity) will mature during the cool season, which is also the aphids' off-season. Your best planting season locally for each of these crops is when the nurseries sell started plants. That, incidentally, is the best way for a novice to start any cole crop. Plant all of them in full sun. Water often; fertilize several times during growth period.

Cabbage

There are early varieties that take 2 to 3 months to mature, and should be spaced 12 inches apart, and late varieties that mature in 3 to 4 months and need 18-inch spacing. As plants grow, mound soil around stems to support tops. Additional roots will grow from the covered stems. Pick cabbages when heads are firm. These round vegetables can be showpieces—red or green leafed kinds. Try one cabbage in a small soy tub for a unique patio container plant.

Brussels sprouts

Don't ever drop the final "s" in Brussels; this vegetable is named for the capital of Belgium. Support stems by mounding during the growing season, as for cabbages. When the big leaves begin to turn yellow, it's time to start picking. Snap off the little sprouts from the bottom first ——they're best when slightly smaller than a golf ball. Leave the little immature sprouts on up the stem to mature. Brussels sprouts continue to produce over a long period; a single plant will yield from 50 to 100 sprouts.

Cauliflower

Of all cole crops, it's the most difficult to grow successfully, but worth a try. It grows best in a cool, moist climate. Daily sprinkling is helpful, especially if a dry, hot spell comes on. The curd, the white part that you eat, doesn't form until toward the end of the growing period. When you see it, fold the outer leaves over the curd and tie them in place to protect it from sun.

Broccoli

This one is very sensitive to heat, especially heat combined with good growing conditions. At first you think it's growing mightily (which it is), but too suddenly you find that the heat has forced it to flower — which means too late for good eating. Pick while heads are tight and not spreading at all. When heads start to spread, stem skins will be thick and need considerable peeling. Pick stems that you need from the base, leaving the less mature ones farther up to develop.

Kale

Imaginative gardeners use this in flower borders and in prominently displayed containers — for its pretty leaves, gray-green or blue-green, curled and corrugated to the point that they look almost unreal. Cooked like spinach or shredded in salad, kale is good but strong in taste. Nurseries seldom sell plants; buy seed and sow it. Plants are easy to transplant. Kale can be grown into summer easier than the others; it doesn't head and isn't so inclined to go to seed in hot weather.

Kohlrabi

Grow this one from seed, too. The eating part is the swollen stem section above ground—good sliced like cucumber.

The potatoes

White (or Irish) potatoes are grown fairly often in gardens. Sweet potatoes take too much space for most places.

Yams and Sweets

These are tropical and so extremely tender crops, for summer growth in hot climates, rich and sandy soil, large spaces. Cut off and plant rooted shoots that grow from temporarily-planted tubers.

White

It takes a sandy, well-drained soil to grow potatoes well. Subsoil should hold moisture. Plant early in spring or in midwinter. Buy certified seed potatoes (they are perfect specimens) at a seed store, cut into chunky pieces ($1\frac{1}{2}$ inches square). Place chunks with eye facing up, 4 inches deep and 18 inches apart. Dig early or "new" potatoes when tops begin to flower. Dig mature potatoes after tops die down.

The solanaceous fruits

As you might guess from the Latin title for this group, they are all related, all belonging to the Solanaceae family. The Solanaceous vegetables (or fruiting vegetables) have these traits in common: All are tender annuals. All are quite widely sold as nursery plants in flats or pots at the right time for local planting (which is just as well; otherwise, standard procedure would call for you to sow the seed and grow it under glass for 8 weeks before the last frost, in order to lengthen the season). Once they come into bearing, all these plants bear their fruits continually until frosts knock them down.

Tomatoes

We know scores of gardeners (chiefly men) whose outstanding achievement each year is growing tomatoes with éclat. If all of these amateur experts could be brought together, they could formulate the ultimate treatise on the skilful culture of garden tomatoes. Meanwhile, some tips to help the not-so-advanced this season: Whether you buy seedlings from the nursery or follow seed packet instructions and grow your own, ideal planting-out size is 2 to 3 inches tall. A dozen plants should supply bountiful tomatoes for the tomato-eatingest family.

Three to six plants supplies plenty for

the usual demand. Plant seedlings at least 3 feet apart; dig holes deep enough to take all of the stems below the first leaves or branches—roots will form there. Pound in a stout 6-foot stake beside each plant; tie stem to it as it grows. Make a water basin immediately, about a foot in diameter (and enlarge it as the plant grows larger). Work a teaspoon of commercial fertilizer into the soil inside the basin. Water. If cutworms are a local problem, put out bait right now. Cultivate to keep weeds out but don't hoe too deep—roots are shallow. Feed according to fertilizer's label directions when immature fruits appear or after first harvest.

Eggplant

It's slow and balky from seed so you'd be wise to buy nursery plants. Set eggplants at the same depth they grew in the flats (not deeper as with tomatoes). Shade young eggplants from sun for a week or so after planting.

Peppers

Pretty leaves, white flowers, and shining green or red peppers on 2 to 2½-foot plants make this crop decorative. Use in a sunny spot as you would a big annual or small shrub.

How to grow healthy tomatoes . . .

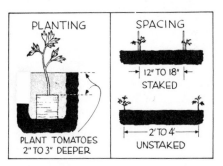

Unlike *most plants, tomatoes are planted deeply. You can bury half the stem.*

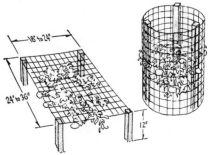

Unstaked *tomatoes need support to keep fruit from rotting on damp ground.*

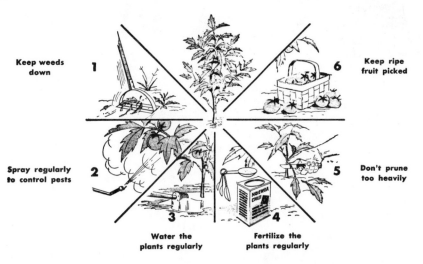

Six-point program *for growing healthy tomatoes:* 1. Weeds compete for moisture and nutrients. Keep them down by shallow cultivation or by mulching. 2. Take steps to control disease even before it is evident; use an all-purpose pesticide. To guard against tobacco mosaic virus, smokers should wash hands with soap and water before handling tomato plants, and not smoke in their vicinity. 3. Soak soil frequently and thoroughly at first; taper off when fruiting starts. 4. Fertilize at least twice during growing season. 5. Hold trimming to a minimum; removing side branches or suckers reduces total yield, causes fruit burn by exposing tomatoes to sun. 6. Plants produce better if fruit is picked frequently and support is provided (see above left, and page 59).

BERRIES

Berries can be among the most rewarding plants in a home garden, but it is important to remember a few basics: Plant only varieties that are suitable to your climate and soil; give them ample growing room, in a sunny location; support tall-growing kinds with a trellis or other suitable training device.

Blackberries. (This group includes not only blackberries but boysenberries, loganberries, youngberries, and nectarberries.) These are deep rooted plants that won't stand shallow, poorly drained soil. To grow as bushes, cut back new canes to 2½ feet in winter; head back resulting laterals to about a foot in early spring (they will be the bearing wood). If you grow them tall, between supporting framework, tip canes back only a foot or so, after they reach 6 feet. (Head laterals the same as in the bush method.) Irrigate deeply and regularly; feed in spring and summer with a balanced fertilizer.

Strawberries. These are easily grown plants that require no special training. They can be grown in any fertile, well-drained soil. Work in plenty of rotted manure prior to planting. Plant in spring; or, if you live in a mild climate, in fall (you'll get berries the first spring). Space 2 to 3 feet apart in rows or raised beds. Strawberries are relatively shallow rooted, so maintain constant moisture in the top 12 inches of soil. Feed with complete fertilizer when fruiting is over and new leaves are beginning to appear.

Raspberries. These do best in regions with a long, cool spring. Long, willowy canes (give them support) don't bear fruit until second year, after which they should be cut to the ground; leave the young, leafy shoots as they will bear fruit for next season.

Grapes. Grape vines are favorites for growing on a trellis or arbor, or against a wall or fence. (If you train them on a wall, make sure they get *afternoon* sun.) Grapes take 3 years to grow to maturity. If planted and pruned properly, watered regularly, and fertilized each year, even a single vine can develop into one of your garden's outstanding features.

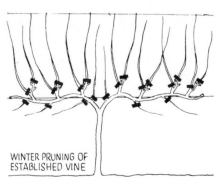

WINTER PRUNING OF ESTABLISHED VINE

Pruning grape. *This shows basic technique for mature plants of most kinds of grape: Cut back to basal buds all shoots that have borne fruit the previous season.*

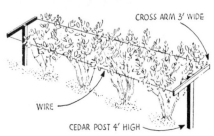

CROSS ARM 3' WIDE
WIRE
CEDAR POST 4' HIGH

Raspberry growers *use supports to hold up new canes after pruning. You could also tip blackberries at 4 or 5 feet, fan them out, and tie them to wires.*

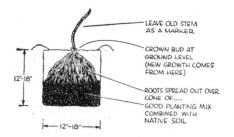

LEAVE OLD STEM AS A MARKER
CROWN BUD AT GROUND LEVEL (NEW GROWTH COMES FROM HERE)
ROOTS SPREAD OUT OVER CONE OF....
GOOD PLANTING MIX COMBINED WITH NATIVE SOIL
12"-18"
12"-18"

Cane berries. *Plant in well-drained, deep soil. Water frequently when plants are in full leaf. Do not fertilize at planting time; wait until roots are established.*

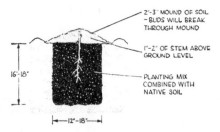

2"-3" MOUND OF SOIL – BUDS WILL BREAK THROUGH MOUND
1"-2" OF STEM ABOVE GROUND LEVEL
PLANTING MIX COMBINED WITH NATIVE SOIL
16"-18"
12"-18"

Grapes. *Bury roots and stem below ground with only the top 1 or 2 inches above ground. You need a deep hole. Tamp soil firmly; water thoroughly.*

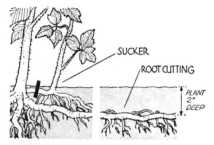

SUCKER
ROOT CUTTING
PLANT 2" DEEP

Suckers, root cuttings *are common ways to propagate blackberries. Raspberries increase by suckers, strawberries by runners or divisions (depends on type).*

Grow strawberries in the ground . . . or in a barrel

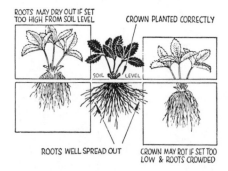

ROOTS MAY DRY OUT IF SET TOO HIGH FROM SOIL LEVEL
CROWN PLANTED CORRECTLY
SOIL LEVEL
ROOTS WELL SPREAD OUT
CROWN MAY ROT IF SET TOO LOW & ROOTS CROWDED

Strawberry crowns *must be at proper level so they won't drown or dry up.*

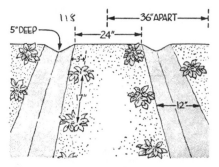

5" DEEP
36" APART
24"
12"

Furrow arrangement *simplifies irrigation if you plant strawberries in rows.*

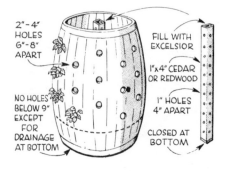

2"-4" HOLES 6"-8" APART
FILL WITH EXCELSIOR
1"x4" CEDAR OR REDWOOD
1" HOLES 4" APART
NO HOLES BELOW 9" EXCEPT FOR DRAINAGE AT BOTTOM
CLOSED AT BOTTOM

Strawberry barrel *is old favorite; center section distributes water laterally.*

CITRUS

In some mild climate regions, orange, lemon, lime, grapefruit and other citrus fruits are very popular.

Adequate *heat* is a must if you are to grow citrus successfully, but only in marginal areas should you plant in full sun. The natural habitat of citrus, contrary to popular belief, is in shade. How much shade or filtered sun they receive varies considerably, depending on variety and subclimate. Rely on the advice of your local nurseryman, not only as to sun but on all cultural matters.

Citrus thrives with intermittent deep watering the year around, but do not overwater. Never plant citrus in or near a lawn, the watering requirements of which will kill them.

Late spring frost, when citrus trees are in a flush of growth, can be murderous. If you grow them in containers, you can deal with this hazard by moving the tubs to a sheltered place. (Container enthusiasts can choose from many excellent dwarf forms.)

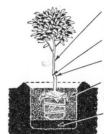

TO PREVENT SUNBURN SHADE TRUNK OR COVER WITH SPECIAL PAINT

KEEP BUD UNION ABOUT 3 INCHES ABOVE GROUND

FACE CUT ON BUD UNION NORTH TO PREVENT SUNBURN

USE PLANTING MIX OF EQUAL PARTS PEAT MOSS, FIR BARK, LOAM

PACK SOIL UNDER ROOT BALL TO PREVENT SETTLING

DIG HOLE DEEP ENOUGH TO GET BELOW HARDPAN, CALICHE

Planting procedure. *To prevent disease, keep top of basin below bud union so water won't reach the trunk.*

HERBS

For gardeners and cooks especially, herbs have a timeless appeal. Their fragrance, flavor, and healing qualities are woven into the rich tapestry of Biblical stories, ancient classics, quaint herbals and scientific works.

Yet with all this background of antiquity, herbs are remarkably up-to-date, free-wheeling plants. Today, few people have space or need for the formal herb gardens of yesteryear, but there's always demand for an attractive and serviceable ground cover, edging, shrub, or container plant. Herbs fill all these needs.

Herbs for the kitchen. A raised bed near the kitchen door, a planter box near the barbecue, or a portion of the vegetable garden makes an ideal location for the herbs you use for cooking and garnishing. Good candidates are chives, chervil, sweet marjoram, spearmint, basil, oregano, parsley, winter savory, rosemary, and common thyme.

Herbs in containers. Use wooden tubs, pots, flue tiles, or almost any kind of container. Herbs that lose their leaves in winter can be moved to an out-of-the-way place during dormancy. Chives and sweet marjoram are excellent types, as are costmary, lemon verbena, orange mint, golden apple mint, garden sage.

Herbs on slopes. Drought-resistant herbs make good soil binders. Common borage is a good tall type (3 feet); prostrate rosemary spreads well and grows to 15 inches high. Silver thyme and lemon thyme are low growers (6-8 inches).

Herbs in perennial or shrub borders. Many of the shrubby herbs combine well with other plants. Examples: sweet woodruff, common wormwood, Roman wormwood, English lavender, lemon verbena, orange mint, golden apple mint, rosemary, and small burnet. Rosemary, lavender, and santolina make fine hedges; plant them on the windward side of the garden so you can catch their fragrance

Culture. Herbs as a group are vigorous, undemanding plants that require only average soil and moisture. Most are sun lovers, but some take part shade.

Lemon thyme *is a popular low grower.*

Sweet marjoram *is "must" for gourmet.*

HANG LEAF HERBS IN LOOSE BRANCHES TO DRY

DRY SEED HERBS ON WIRE SCREEN OR MUSLIN

IF MOISTURE APPEARS ON INSIDE OF GLASS JAR, HERBS ARE NOT THOROUGHLY DRY

Store dried herbs *in airtight containers.*

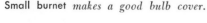

Small burnet *makes a good bulb cover.*

Golden apple mint *prefers part shade.*

Chives *are perennial culinary favorite.*

SUCCULENTS

The name "succulent" is derived from the Latin *succulentus,* which means juicy or fleshy, and the term is applied to all drought-resistant plants especially adapted to taking up and storing great quantities of water in their leaves, stems, and branches. Succulents are found in the cactus, lily, pineapple, amaryllis, agave, carpetweed, stonecrop, spurge, milkweed, and sunflower families of plants.

Success with succulents requires an understanding of where they came from and how they were meant to develop and grow. Succulents are found in every part of the world where plants have difficulty in getting and keeping water—particularly in desert and high mountain regions where soil is lean and the sandy soil drains rapidly.

Cuttings *are good way to start many succulents (this is Mexican sedum). Clockwise from the upper right: long cuttings to plant out; short ones to start in flat; rooted plants; older rooted stems.*

Divisions *of many clump-forming types can be made every year or two. Each new division will start a new clump. Plant them so the base is level with surface of the soil. This is Echeveria elegans.*

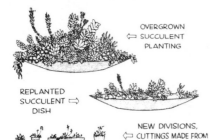

Occasional *dividing and replanting keeps succulents looking good. Divide in early summer when new growth starts.*

To duplicate the conditions of their natural habitat as closely as possible, plant them where they get ample sunlight (they will tolerate some shade); use a mix of 2 parts coarse sand, 1 part loam, 1 part leaf mold, and ½ part granulated charcoal. Water very sparingly the year around, letting soil dry out between waterings. Overwatering can cause succulents to rot, as well as harming them in many other ways.

Drainage in pots or beds must be perfect. In making a bed for succulents, raise it above the ground level entirely. First lay 3 or 4 inches of crushed rock or pea gravel as a base for drainage, then add the soil mix over it at least 6 inches deep. Sink some large rocks into the soil to form interesting contours for planting.

Although there are a few hardy examples such as sempervivum and sedum, most succulents are tender plants. In cold climates, grow in pots or other containers, and move them to a well-lighted indoor location for winter. If you live in a region where winters are mild, you can grow them either in containers or in permanent outdoor locations.

ALOE STRIATA
Orange-red blooms; dramatic.

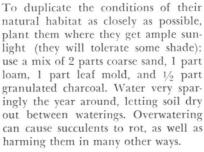

DUDLEYA
White, luminous leaves.

KALANCHOE
Leaves have silky hairs.

SEMPERVIVUM TECTORUM
Called "hen-and-chickens."

CRASSULA PERFOLIATA
An outstanding pot plant.

COTYLEDON ORBICULATA
Gray leaves edged with red.

SENECIO SCAPOSUS
Leaves are like soft felt.

CONOPHYTUM PLACITUM
One of the "pebble plants."

BAMBOO

Bamboo is a much more versatile plant than is generally realized, ranging from dwarf types only 10 inches tall to giants that sometimes grow as high as 80 feet. There are types for both warm and cold climates.

Once it has taken several years to become established, bamboo is among the world's fastest-growing plants. This, in addition to the evergreen leaves, makes bamboo an excellent choice for screen plantings.

Both clump types and running types are available. *Clump types* are limited in their horizontal root expansion and are not invasive. *Running* types send out long rhizomes from which emerge new vertical stems; over the years, they can run rampant if uncontrolled. To confine them, use dividers of galvanized sheet metal set 18 inches deep around the plant; or grow in containers.

Many kinds of bamboo (both clump and running types) make exotic tub subjects. You'll have to divide them every 3 to 5 years as follows:

Wait until May or June, when new sprouts are appearing. Lay grasp to a few stems and pull steadily as you tap around the rim with a mallet or hammer. When the root ball is removed, cut it right down the center with a spade or axe. Plant the halves in fresh soil; or, if you want 4 plants, cut each half in two and then replant.

CULTURE

Plant bamboo in full sun or partial shade. Any reasonably good soil will do. Set running types at a depth of 6 inches; on clump or dwarf varieties, plant with only the roots beneath the soil. Keep bamboo well watered. Mulching is beneficial, as is an occasional feeding with a slow-acting fertilizer.

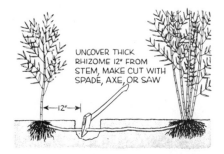
Running type: *To divide, cut rhizome; dig plant with a good ball of soil.*

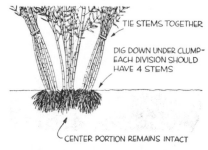
Clump type: *Increases like a hardy perennial, divides easily with spade.*

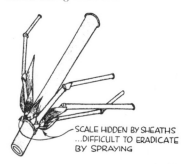
To control scale, *spray with malathion in spring; combine with oil in fall.*

GROUND COVERS

Time was when the only ground cover most of us considered was turf grass. Then we broadened the definition to include Irish moss and ivy. In recent years, with increased emphasis on low maintenance gardens, the list has grown to include a seemingly endless variety of low growing perennials, shrubs, and vines. Here are a few uses and suggestions:

Soil-binders for sunny slopes. Hall's honeysuckle, prostrate rosemary, ivy, *Hypericum calycinum, Ceanothus gloriosus,* helianthemum, *Arctostaphylos uva-ursi,* hybrid brooms, and various forms of dwarf juniper.

Between stepping stones. Choose close-cropped plants that hug the ground. Mother-of-thyme, wooly thyme, Irish moss, and chamomile are excellent. In California, dichondra is popular for this purpose and also as a lawn substitute (it can be planted from flats or you can sow seed).

Problem spots. Nepeta, ajuga, and pachysandra are among the many flowering ground covers that can improve the appearance of an awkward, hard-to-get-at area.

Vertical elements, *placed in flat, one-tone ground covers, prevent a pavement-like sameness. Examples: Nandina with dwarf plumbago, shrubs or small trees with ivy.*

You need not buy *as many plants if you space ground covers 2 or 3 feet apart and—while they are spreading—fill the bare ground with low growing annuals.*

FERNS

Many ferns, the natural undergrowth of our forests, make themselves right at home in the garden. There are all kinds, from shoe-top height to tree size. They are remarkably easy to grow, and they can serve a variety of garden uses.

Plant ferns in late winter or early spring in soil that will hold moisture yet drain well—the same kind of soil demanded by begonias, fuchsias, and acid-loving shrubs. Equal parts leaf mold, loam, and peat moss is a good medium.

Allow ferns plenty of root room. Space them so fronds touch but don't interlace; some ferns have roots that spread out 3 feet or more. Don't plant them too deep because the roots range in the top few inches of soil.

Most ferns prefer shade but, with the exception of some tiny alpines, will also grow in the open. Watering needs vary somewhat depending on their environment.

Line a shady garden path with them. Sword fern, maidenhair, or any fern that is fairly compact growing will be a reminder to stay on the path, yet won't block the view beyond.

Or plant ferns in drifts on a shady bank, and interplant with primroses or bold-foliaged bergenia (saxifrage).

Use them as a textured carpet under trees, or as transition plants between garden and woods. Or contrast foliages: lacy ferns against plants with broad or narrow leaves.

We have even seen ferns used very effectively as "lazy man's foundation planting" along the north side of a house.

Cut back *old fronds in late winter when the new growth starts to unfurl.*

Ferns make good container plants. Keep several in tubs to fill in bare spots in the shade, or group them on a shady terrace, with tubbed hydrangeas or tuberous begonias in full flower.

Remember that ferns growing in containers need ample root space. When you repot your ferns, always use a pot that is two sizes larger than the present container.

INDOOR PLANTS

The growing of indoor plants—African violets, orchids, dieffenbachia, and countless others—is one of the most fascinating of all garden subjects. Your choices in plants are so many and varied that to make even a representative list would require many pages.

Actually, the world of indoor plants is an entirely different one from that of the garden plants we are chiefly concerned with in this book. We can, however, make one observation which the would-be indoor gardener might well heed: Throw out the rule book so far as culture of most garden plants is concerned. For every general rule that may hold true for outdoor and indoor plants alike, there's another which does not.

Success in growing plants indoors depends more on how well you control the moisture supply than on any other factor. Use one of the commercial indoor planting mixes. Keep it moist but not saturated; always wait just until it dries out before watering again. Generally, you'll water smaller containers twice weekly; large containers every week or two.

Sufficient light is another vital factor. A position near a north window is usually ideal. Keep the house temperature as consistent as possible. Above all, keep them out of the sun.

A monthly feeding with diluted liquid fertilizer is beneficial. Keep leaves free of house dust. Occasional washing will keep plants free of tiny insects.

DEARBORN-MASSAR

Splitleaf philodendron *makes a dramatic indoor subject in a floor planter. Tall bamboo grows alongside at right.*

BLAIR STAPP

Use glass bowls, *brandy snifters as planters. Plant in dry vermiculite, then water; it will remain damp for months.*

Transplanting the tiny ones . . .

Put dry mix in dish, *then scoop out a place to receive roots of first plant. Work dirt off roots so it will fit (won't hurt most tiny house plants if done with care).*

BLAIR STAPP

Little planter *with specimens from photograph at left, plus bigger planting made at same time. Use plastic clothes sprinkler or a syringe; always water gently.*

CHAPTER 13

Using Plants Effectively

DARROW M. WATT

- Landscaping with flowers under trees, along fences, next to parking areas and driveways, beneath windows, in borders, beside pools; planting for dramatic or unusual effect; combining plants, forms, and colors: pages 124 and 125

LANDSCAPING WITH FLOWERS

The planting suggestions on these two pages are intended to suggest ideas for using plants in typical home garden situations. Not all plants shown will grow in all climates. For our purposes, this is perhaps more of a help than a hindrance—at least if it will help you to remember a fundamental rule of successful landscaping: *Choose plants that are your own particular favorites and that are adapted to your climate.*

If you have any kind of an eye for color and plant form, the variations on any one of the schemes shown here are virtually endless.

For example, the lotus (a tender plant) spilling over the retaining wall could just as well be *Convolvulus mauritani-* *cus,* if you live in a cold-winter region. It could be any number of other plants with similar characteristics, for that matter.

Color selection, as well as climate adaptability, is a variable. Perhaps you don't like pastels; maybe, for some reason, you don't care for yellow and red combinations. Whatever your dislikes, you'll find that there are many other colors (perhaps in other varieties of the same plant) that suit your taste.

If you have a scheme in mind but, like most gardeners, your knowledge of plants is pretty well limited to what you've grown in the past, ask a reliable nurseryman what he would use to achieve the desired effect.

Under a flowering cherry, *astilbe adds a soft, frothy touch around a solid mass of pink and white hydrangeas.*

In a front parking area, *violas combine with iris. Even after plants flower, iris foliage continues to look attractive.*

Tropical effect: *Castor bean is background for yucca's sword-shaped foliage; dwarf yellow marigolds grow below.*

Along a fence, *spikes of yellow snapdragons rise in front of blue morning glory; blue petunias in foreground.*

Gay streetside planting *combines sun-loving dimorphotheca (white), red verbena, and drifts of white alyssum.*

In a shady poolside border, *lush green leaves of hosta make an effective frame for white lacecap hydrangeas.*

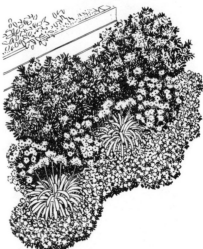

Along a garden fence, *white oleander is fronted by Shasta daisy, blue agapanthus, dwarf phlox in pastels.*

Along a shaded drive *in wind-protected spot, Australian tree fern, calla, ajuga ground cover make lush scene.*

Over retaining wall: *Gray lotus (or Convolvulus mauritanicus), blue lobelia along edge; white impatiens behind.*

Under birches, *Oriental hellebore's bushy, substantial form is contrasted with graceful, airy effect of coral bells.*

In front of a window, *handsome foliaged, white flowering* Skimmia japonica *behind coral bells. Shady exposure.*

In a seaside garden, *artichoke used as ornamental shrub with flowery complement of* Zephyranthes candida.

Variety along a fence: *Red begonias under birches offer lively contrast with yellow roses (floribundas, climbers).*

Along a garden path, *blue agapanthus rises out of carpet of yellow gazanias; rice paper plant in the background.*

Next to a sunny driveway, *dwarf red Michaelmas daisies grow in front of Japanese barberry; plum trees behind.*

In a wide border, *front to rear: white alyssum, yellow dwarf marigolds, yellow chrysanthemums, and orange dahlias.*

Index

Page numbers in boldface type refer to illustrations of the primary subject. After plant names, boldface indicates an illustration of the plant or one of its components.